Math Meets Markets

Math Meets Markets

The Unwritten Rules of Quant Life

First Edition

Kambiz Homayounfar

Nippotica Corporation
Tokyo, Japan

Some examples and visualizations in this book were created using Wolfram Mathematica, a computational software system developed by Wolfram Research, Inc. The Mathematica code snippets included herein are original or adapted by the author for illustrative and educational purposes only.

ISBN: 978-4-911671-01-6

Printed in the United States of America

"*A good quant must be a mixture, too—part trader, part salesperson, part programmer, and part mathematician.*"
—Emanuel Derman, My Life as a Quant: Reflections on Physics and Finance (Derman, 2012)

"*Keep computations to the lowest level of the multiplication table.*"
—David Hilbert

Contents

	List of Figures	ix
	List of Tables	xi
	List of Acronyms	xiii
	Listings	xv
	Preface	xvii
1	**The Quant's Dilemma** Genius or Grunt Work?	1
2	**The Holy Trinity** Models, Data, and Assumptions	9
3	**Stochastic Wizardry** What They Didn't Teach You in School	15
4	**Modeling vs. Trading** The Ivory Tower Meets the Bloodbath	27
5	**Risk** The Four-Letter Word That Runs the World	37
6	**Backtesting** The Art of Fooling Yourself with Style	51
7	**Socratic Finance** Dialogs on Bugs, Precision, and Accuracy	65
8	**AI in Finance** A Trader's-Eye View from Inside the Machine	77

9 **The Mirage of the Mean** 87
The Dangerous Charm of Averages

10 **Quant Survival and Beyond** 95
How to Stay Sharp, Stay Sane, and Eventually Move On

A **Wolfram for the Functionally Curious** 107
Guiding the Pythonically Perplexed

B **Why You Should Write in Mathematica** 117
Even If Everyone Else Is on Python

C **Mathematica Code Snippets** 123

Glossary 135
Bibliography 139
Index 141

List of Figures

3.1 GBM vs. Merton's Jumpy Paths: (a) A path of a GBM process with $r = 0.1$ and $\sigma = 1.0$. This single GBM path appears as continuous, smooth, and jump-free—unlike anything you'd encounter in real markets. (b) Two sample paths of the Merton jump diffusion model with drift $\mu = 0.2$, volatility $\sigma = 0.7$, and jump intensity $\lambda = 3$. The simulation covers a 1-year horizon with daily time steps ($\Delta t = 0.01$) and shows the two sample trajectories. 16

3.2 The Kou Model: (a) Simulated path of the Kou jump-diffusion model with parameters: $s_0 = 100$, $\mu = 0.05$, $\sigma = 0.2$, $\lambda = 0.1$, $p = 0.5$, $\eta_1 = 0.1$, $\eta_2 = 0.1$, $T = 1$, $n = 1000$, $\Delta t = 0.001$. (b) QQ plot of log returns simulated from the Kou jump-diffusion model, with excess kurtosis $k_e = -0.061968$. 19

3.3 Empirical distributions of simulated jump sizes under Merton's normal model (left) and Kou's double exponential model (right). The vertical dashed lines at ±10% highlight how frequently large downside moves occur under Kou's asymmetric structure. 21

3.4 Two well-known securities: Gold and the S&P500 Index 21

3.5 Snapshots of the log returns of two well-known securities: Gold and the S&P500 Index 22

3.6 Histograms of the log returns of two well-known securities: Gold and the S&P500 Index 22

3.7 QQ plots help to visualize the long tails: note the upward and downward deviations in the tails where extreme returns occur more often than the Gaussian benchmark would predict. 23

5.1 Dow Jones Industrial Average levels during major crash events: 1987, 1998, 2008, and 2020. The scale and speed of these drawdowns highlight the limitations of models assuming normally distributed returns. 41

5.2 Black Monday October 1987: Peak and Trough of DJIA 41

6.1 Bitcoin Price in US$: 2019-2025 59

6.2 The six regime changes in Bitcoin since 2019. Note that the price axes are adjusted to match. 61

6.3 Jackknifed Returns (a) S&P500 index during in 2020 Covid Pandemic, and (b) Range of the annual return of a S&P500 buy-and-hold strategy. The min, med, and max of the annual return are marked. Vertical dashed lines shown the 1% and 99% quantiles. 62

7.1 Comparison of two equivalent expressions over a small domain around $x = 0$. While mathematically equivalent, (a) suffers from catastrophic cancellation for small x, resulting in significant numerical error. The reformulated version shown in (b) maintains stability and preserves precision across the domain. 68

A.1 Using `Manipulate` to display parabolas. 113

A.2 Using `Manipulate` to display integer factors. 113

A.3 Using `Manipulate` to display traveling waves. 114

A.4 Using `Dynamic` for real-time updates to a plot. 115

List of Tables

4.1 When Size Starts to Hurt: Nonlinear Execution Costs 30
5.1 Maximum Drawdown of DJIA for Black Monday 1987 42
6.1 Backtest Assumptions vs. Live Trading Realities 52
6.2 Strategy returns across volatility regimes. 58
6.3 Bitcoin price regimes from 2019 to 2025. 59
8.1 ML vs. DL in Practice 79
8.2 AI Use Cases in Trading 80

List of Acronyms

AI Artificial Intelligence

CVaR Conditional Value-at-Risk

DJIA Dow Jones Industrial Average

DL Deep Learning

ETF Exchange-Traded Fund

FoF Fund of Funds

FOMO Fear of Missing Out

LSTM Long Short-Term Memory

LTCM Long Term Capital Management

MCMC Markov Chain Monte Carlo

MDD Maximum Drawdown

ML Machine Learning

NaN Not a Number

NLP Natural Language Processing

PCA Principal Component Analysis

PM Portfolio Manager

PnL	Profit And Loss
QQ	Quantile-Quantile
SABR	Stochastic Alpha-Beta-Rho
SDE	Stochastic Differential Equation
SPDR	Standard & Poor's Depositary Receipts
WL	Wolfram Language
VaR	Value-at-Risk
XAI	Explainable AI

Listings

C.1 Code for Figure 3.1a 123
C.2 Code for Figure 3.1b 123
C.3 Code for Figure 3.3 124
C.4 Code for Figure 3.4 125
C.5 Code for Figure 3.5 125
C.6 Code for Figure 3.6 125
C.7 Code for Figure 3.7 126
C.8 Code for Figure 5.1 127
C.9 Code for Figure 5.2 128
C.10 Code for Table 5.1 128
C.11 Code for Figure 6.3a 130
C.12 Code for Figure 6.3b 130
C.13 Code for Algorithm 1 132
C.14 Code for Figure 7.1a 133
C.15 Code for Figure 7.1b 133

Preface

Quantitative finance sits at the intersection of math, code, and markets. On the surface it looks polished—driven by logic, powered by data, tuned for precision. Bright minds build sleek models, and profits seem to follow. That's the brochure. The reality is messier. Strategies break. Data misleads. Models buckle under stress. The market is indifferent to elegance; it only rewards what works.

Forget learning Itô's lemma step by step. Forget exotic option pricing formulas or tricks for taming a pandas dataframe. You won't find a QuantLib manual here, and you won't slog through a treatise on stochastic calculus. What you will find is a survival guide. A field notebook from someone who has stumbled, scribbled lessons in the margins, and kept moving forward.

Before I go further, let's define the job. A "quant"—short for quantitative analyst—is someone who builds models, writes code, analyzes noise disguised as data, and tries to find structure in the chaos of financial markets. Quants are supposed to joggle theory and trade, sometimes closer to one, often crushed between both. Some build pricing models. Some write algorithms. Some debug what others broke. The job looks cleaner on paper than it feels in practice.

This book is about that feeling—the lived reality of being a quant. It's more than money, math, and logic. It's long hours, odd bugs, confusing meetings, and the occasional, inexplicable success. Being wrong often. Being right just enough. Learning to live in the gap between the two.

Who Should Read This Book? If you're exploring the world of quantitative finance—as a student, an aspiring quant, or a trader trying to decode the black-box world—this book is for you.

If you're early in your career, consider this a roadmap, not just through technical terrain but through the politics, pitfalls, and cultural quirks of finance firms. If you're already in the trenches, think of it as a mirror: honest, sometimes unflattering, but familiar.

I assume you know some math, some code, and some finance. But I don't bury you in notation. The point here is clarity, not intimidation. Good quants explain well. This book aims to do the same.

What This Book Covers I walk through the quant life—from your first day in the industry to the moment you start wondering what comes after. The chapters balance technical ideas with human realities. Each one focuses on a core challenge, a recurring trap, or a piece of practical wisdom.

Chapter 1 The Quant's Dilemma explores the reality of what quants actually do, dispelling the myth that it is all about intellectual elegance. The truth is a mix of high-level mathematics and low-level debugging.

Chapter 2 The Holy Trinity covers the three fundamental pillars of quant work. Models matter, but bad data and flawed assumptions can ruin even the most mathematically sound strategies.

Chapter 3 Stochastic Wizardry discusses why financial markets defy standard probability models, why volatility is never constant, and why stochastic calculus is a beautiful but flawed tool.

Chapter 4 Trading vs. Modeling dives into the disconnect between quants and traders. A great model does not automatically make money. Implementation, execution, and trader psychology matter just as much.

Chapter 5 Risk examines the real meaning of risk, why standard measures like volatility are misleading, and how catastrophic market events always defy probability models.

Chapter 6 Backtesting reveals why most backtests lie, how overfitting seduces even experienced quants, and why transaction costs, liquidity, and regime shifts destroy theoretically profitable strategies.

Chapter 7 The Greeks explains delta, gamma, vega, theta, and rho not as abstract mathematical concepts, but as forces that drive options markets in real time.

Chapter 8 AI in Finance a trader's-eye critique of AI in quantitative finance, where black-box models meet human instinct, and the real question is whether we can still see the market clearly. Spoiler: It's complicated!

Chapter 9 The Mirage of Means reminds us that in markets, the average is often the least representative outcome—like measuring the height of a mountain range by its mean elevation and forgetting the cliffs that break climbers.

Chapter 10 Beyond the Terminal examines why few quants stay in finance forever, the common exit paths, and how to transition into roles in portfolio management, fintech, research, or entrepreneurship.

All figures in this book were generated using the Wolfram Language (Mathematica), which was chosen for its clarity, symbolic power, and ease of visualization. To help readers explore, adapt, or extend these visualizations, three appendices provide an overview of the language (Appendix A), a rationale for using it in quant work (Appendix B), and code snippets for all key examples (Appendix C).

How to Use This Book Read straight through, or skip around. New to quant work? Start with models, risk, and backtesting. Already a veteran? Go to the chapters on office survival and life after "quanting."

I keep jargon to a minimum and intuition up front. There are plenty of papers full of proofs. This book is about what happens when those proofs meet real-world constraints.

Quantitative finance is full of contradictions. It demands precision and rewards adaptability. It's rooted in logic but shaped by people. It's technical, but not purely technical.

The best quants combine sharp code and elegant models with deep understanding of the context they operate in. They see the game. They know that alpha is temporary, politics are permanent, and survival is underrated.

This book is for those who want more than just theory. It's for those who want to think, adapt, and maybe even thrive.

Welcome to the real quant life.

Kambiz Homayounfar
September, 2025

1 The Quant's Dilemma

Genius or Grunt Work?

On his first day, the new quant expected a market model. What he got was a Perl script from 1997 and a mandate to "make it work." This was a mission-critical project driving the daily risk reports for a billion-dollar trading desk. When he asked for documentation, his manager chuckled and said, "If we had documentation, we wouldn't need you."

Welcome to quantitative finance, where the job description promises stochastic calculus but delivers legacy code and trading floor diplomacy. The seduction starts with theory—Gaussian distributions, Brownian motion, no arbitrage—but once you're in, you learn that it's less about solving equations and more about surviving chaos. To understand that chaos, you need to know where quants actually operate — and how wildly that terrain can vary.

Between Ivory and Asphalt

The gap between academic theory and trading floor reality gets bridged by the most precarious infrastructure imaginable. Somewhere between the ivory tower and the asphalt jungle sits a digital house of cards: shell scripts written at 3 AM, quick fixes that became permanent, and documentation that exists only in the institutional memory of people who've already quit.

Quants who work on risk management spend their days building levees against financial floods, knowing that every model they create is just another sandbag in an endless war against market chaos. Trading desk quants debug execution algorithms while voices boom across the floor about spreads that moved three basis points in the wrong direction. Research quants wrestle with models that work beautifully in backtests but fall apart the moment real money touches them, then present their findings to portfolio managers who've seen it all before.

"If there were documentation, you wouldn't have a job."

None of this resembles the Hollywood version of quantitative finance. There's no genius quietly scribbling equations on a whiteboard while millions pour into his account. Instead, there's a programmer at 2 AM trying to figure out why the overnight batch jobs failed, a risk manager explaining to senior management why their VaR model didn't predict yesterday's losses, and a researcher discovering that her breakthrough strategy stops working the moment she scales it up.

The mythology persists because it's more appealing than the truth. Clean mathematics, elegant solutions, intellectual mastery over chaotic markets—these stories sell better than the reality of patching legacy systems and explaining why sophisticated models still can't predict what happens when central banks get creative.

But this unglamorous work keeps the financial world spinning. Every quick fix, every late-night debugging session, every model that works just well enough to make it through another trading day—this is the real backbone of quantitative finance.

Where Quants Fit in the Machine

Before we go further, it helps to know the different kinds of quants you'll meet—or become. The titles blur, and people move between them, but the broad shapes look like this.

Modeling quants build the pricing and risk models. They live in SDEs, calibrations, and factor structures. Their work sets the theoretical framework for valuing trades and measuring exposure.

Desk quants sit with traders and integrate models into the day-to-day workflow. They adapt theoretical outputs into something usable under time pressure, making sure the model's numbers appear in the right place, at the right time, on the right screen.

Execution quants optimize the mechanics of getting into and out of trades. They wrestle with slippage, market impact, and order-routing logic—turning a theoretical signal into an actual fill at a competitive price.

Research quants explore new strategies, datasets, and statistical edges. They run experiments, mine historical data, and stress-test hypotheses. Sometimes their work flows into production; sometimes it dies quietly in a backtest folder.

In practice, these roles overlap. A desk quant may design new execution logic; a modeling quant might drift into research. But knowing the archetypes gives you a map. Later, when I talk about bug-fixing at 2 AM or arguing with a trader about liquidity, you'll know which corner of the map we're standing in.

The Illusion of Genius

There's a myth in finance: that genius alone crafts elegant models, markets fall in line, and money simply follows. Reality, of course, is less theatrical. In practice, the early years often mean cleaning datasets, chasing misaligned timestamps between New York and London, and wondering why your Monte Carlo simulation returns `NaN` after the quarterly data refresh.

Quants write and code formulas, yes—but more importantly, they keep those formulas from combusting under the weight of a production system that no one fully understands. You might know how to derive a closed-form solution to the SABR model, but you'll spend more time figuring out why the data feed is stuck on yesterday. And when you finally get the model running, another truth waits around the corner: it's going to break.

The Model Always Breaks

There's a quiet panic behind every model. Everyone knows it's wrong. The job is knowing where and when it breaks. Traders want numbers that hold up under pressure. When volatility spikes and the model fails, they don't ask why—they just say "fix it."

Take Black-Scholes: elegant in form, undeniably influential, and fundamentally flawed. It assumes continuous trading, lognormal returns, zero transaction costs — a world that doesn't exist. Still, the model endures. The model endures because it's tractable—clear, manageable, and useful for making decisions, even if its assumptions are simplified. Easy to calibrate. Easy to justify. So quants patch it. They tweak vol surfaces, add correction terms, inject heuristics. The math stays clean on paper, but the implementation becomes a negotiation with reality.

The fall of LTCM in 1998 is often told as a cautionary tale about leverage, but at its core, it was a story about overconfidence in elegant math. The firm was a quant's dream—Nobel laureates at the helm, models rooted in sophisticated stochastic calculus, and a belief that arbitrage could be systematized with enough precision. For a while, it worked. Their models identified tiny mispricings across global bond markets, and with enormous leverage, they turned those slivers into profits.

Then came the Russian debt crisis. Investors across the world fled risk, liquidity vanished, and correlations between supposedly independent assets snapped into lockstep. The models hadn't accounted for what happens when everyone runs for the same exit at once. The assumptions—normal distributions, orderly markets, independence of events—were mathematically neat, but psychologically naive.

Traders responded to fear. Spreads widened, positions became impossible to unwind, and the very market structure the model depended on ceased to function.

When LTCM collapsed, the mathematics remained sound, but the model faced a market-wide panic that exceeded every assumption built into it. The framework had been calibrated for orderly markets, liquid positions, and stable correlations. In the crisis, those foundations vanished. Liquidity evaporated, correlations converged, and asset prices moved in ways the model had no mechanism to capture. It was the shock of an environment the equations had never been designed to survive.

The Seduction of Backtesting

A good backtest feels like proof. Sharpe ratios gleam, equity curves rise smoothly, and the model seems bulletproof. But behind that polished result is often a leak: data contamination, overfitting, or some other quiet sabotage that only shows itself when real money is at stake.

Every quant has that moment—the model looks spectacular until it doesn't. Eventually, you learn to treat every backtest as a minefield. The trick is less about perfection, and more about a clear sense of where the landmines are likely buried.

Market Truths, Trader Questions

Eigenvalues rarely settle a trade. What traders need is a hedge, a clear signal, a line of reasoning they can act on in the next two minutes. A quant's value lies not in being theoretically right, but in being usable when the market demands clarity.

Even the most robust model will be greeted with a shrug if it doesn't help make decisions. The job involves turning complex ideas into something others can actually use. If your output doesn't survive contact with a caffeine-charged desk and a twitchy market open, you built the wrong thing.

IQ ≠Alpha

Markets judge you on PnL rather than your academic credentials. You can have three PhDs and still get schooled by a trader running Excel macros held together with duct tape and prayer. The market rewards what works, period.

One day you're frantically recalibrating your sophisticated volatility model because overnight spreads[1] jumped in ways that violate every assumption you've built your career on. The next day, some guy on the trading floor is beating your carefully crafted algorithm with a spreadsheet that crashes every time he opens it. His secret weapon? Ten years of watching how bonds behave when the Federal Reserve chair clears his throat during press conferences.

Finance pretends to be a meritocracy, but really it's more like a demolition derby. Beautiful theories get crushed by ugly realities. Elegant mathematics lose to brute-force pattern recognition. The trader who can't spell "stochastic" might be the one making money while a rocket scientist explains to the

[1] An overnight spread jump is what happens when the bid-ask spread—the tiny gap between what buyers are willing to pay and what sellers want to get—suddenly becomes not-so-tiny after the market closes and before it reopens.

boss why a Nobel Prize-worthy model just lost a fortune on a currency move that shouldn't have been possible.

"Your IQ is below my alpha!"

Your degree might open a door, but your PnL keeps it open. Intelligence matters in finance, but only if you can back it up with numbers. You can be the smartest person in the room and still get shown the exit if your trades don't work. Markets measure success in profits, not potential, and the scoreboard resets every day. That's why the people who last aren't just clever — they know how to turn insight into performance that shows up in the ledger.

Quants thrive when they produce results; the formulas are just tools along the way. You can derive Black-Scholes from memory, but the market doesn't hand out bonuses for elegance on paper. It rewards those who use their tools to generate returns in the real world. The market is the ultimate judge, and it has zero interest in your academic credentials when it's deciding whether to make you rich or send you home. In the end, it's a brutally fair game: you either make it money, or you don't.

A Beautiful, Broken Game

Quantitative finance is messy by design. It's a game played in a fog, with broken tools and unreliable data. It rewards those who adapt, who debug in silence and explain in plain language. The dilemma lies in navigating the messy space where theory meets practice—and figuring out how to survive there.

A junior quant once joined a well-known trading desk straight out of a math PhD program. Brilliant, confident, fluent in SDEs—he was convinced that with enough rigor, any market problem could be solved. On his first week, he proudly shared a volatility arbitrage model that had passed every stress test he could throw at it. The head trader listened, nodded, then handed him a list of bugs in the code. Half of them had nothing to do with math—just bad data feeds, server sync issues, and a timezone mismatch that no theorem could fix.[2]

A month later, the model was abandoned. The math held up fine, but the model collapsed under the pressure of the real trading environment.

[2] In this chapter I stayed clear of stochastic calculus for a reason. The first lie every quant learns is that math will save you. What does the saving, more often, is resilience.

2 The Holy Trinity

Models, Data, and Assumptions

Knight Capital's death spiral lasted forty-five minutes. (Austin and Meister, 2015) In that time, a ghost in their system—old code that should have been buried—came back to life and started hurling orders at the market like a drunk trader with unlimited credit. The firm lost $440 million before anyone could pull the plug.

The engineers at Knight were skilled professionals—well-versed in risk management, system architecture, and all the core technical fundamentals. But they had made a quiet assumption that proved fatal: they believed their own system. They trusted that decommissioned code would stay dead, that their safeguards would catch anomalies, that decades of incremental patches and updates hadn't left any digital landmines buried in the codebase.

This assumption killed them faster than any mathematical error ever could have.

Every trading system runs on three pillars that most people never think about explicitly. First, the models—the mathematical frameworks that try to make sense of market behavior. Second, the data—the endless streams of prices, volumes, and signals that feed those models. Third, the assumptions—the quiet beliefs about how everything should work together.

These assumptions are everywhere. They live in the code that decides when to execute trades, in the risk controls that are supposed to prevent disasters, in the basic faith that yesterday's working system will still work today. Mathematical models get tested endlessly. Data gets scrubbed and validated. But assumptions? They hide in plain sight, invisible until they detonate.

Knight Capital learned this the hard way. Their models were fine. Their data was clean. But their assumption that old code stays dead turned out to be spectacularly wrong, and it cost them everything.

The Model Is Only One-Third of the Battle

Every financial model carries the DNA of its creators—their assumptions about how markets should behave, their understanding of risk, their beliefs about human nature. Markets, meanwhile, operate according to their own twisted logic, which changes without warning and rarely sends a memo.

Consider Black-Scholes, the granddaddy of options pricing. Academics love to point out its flaws: markets have friction, volatility jumps around like a caffeinated squirrel, and liquidity has this annoying habit of vanishing precisely when you need it most. Yet traders use it every day to price billions in derivatives. They've learned to treat it like a rough translation rather than gospel truth—tweaking it with implied volatility, adjusting for real-world messiness, bending it to fit the chaos they actually encounter.

The beauty lies in this adaptation. Traders use Black-Scholes as a foundation—starting with its structure, then refining it through corrections, adjustments, and expert judgment to make it practical and effective. The original mathematical elegance gets buried under practical modifications, but the core framework survives.

Most model failures happen when circumstances shift but the assumptions stay frozen in time. Yesterday's clean data reveals hidden glitches. Market relationships that seemed permanent dissolve overnight. The model structure might be perfectly sound, but it's solving the wrong problem—answering questions about a market that no longer exists.

Data Carries the Hidden Knife

Bad data creeps in like carbon monoxide—odorless, invisible, deadly. A timestamp gets shifted by a few milliseconds. A server in Singapore pulls yesterday's closing price while another in London uses today's opening tick. Currency conversions lag by thirty seconds during volatile sessions. The system keeps humming along, generating numbers that look perfectly reasonable until someone bothers to dig deeper.

Consider the junior quant who stumbled across a billion-dollar puzzle. (Lindsey and Schachter, 2009) The derivatives desk was pricing their book one way, his models were spitting out different numbers, and nobody could explain the gap. Turns out two servers were pulling from volatility surfaces that had diverged weeks earlier—one updated, one frozen in time. The math was identical. The data was just slightly, catastrophically different.

This happens more often than anyone wants to admit. Trades get executed based on prices that are seconds old. Risk calculations use exchange rates from the previous day's close. Portfolio valuations drift because one feed rounds to four decimal places while another uses six. Each error seems trivial in isolation, but they compound like interest, creating phantom profits and invisible losses that only surface when someone finally asks the right questions.

The insidious part is how normal everything looks. The screens glow with their usual confidence. The algorithms churn through their calculations. The reports get generated on schedule. Meanwhile, the foundation is slowly rotting away, one corrupted data point at a time.

One way to catch these early is to compare the same data from two independent sources each day and flag any differences that are bigger than you're willing to accept.

Assumptions Don't Show Up in the Output

Wall Street has a dirty little secret: the smartest people in the room are often undone by the things they never bother to write down.

Take one hedge fund I advised—let's call them Smart Money Capital. They ran a mean-reversion strategy that made quants weep with joy. Two assets had moved in lockstep for years, drifting apart and snapping back like they were joined by an invisible rubber band. Backtests were gorgeous. Early returns were even better.

Then, one day, the rubber band snapped. Not with a crash—just a quiet, steady drift that never reversed. The correlation they had treated as gravity simply evaporated. The models were fine. The code was fine. What failed was the belief that yesterday's relationship would hold tomorrow. By the time they realized the assumption was gone, the portfolio was already bleeding.

Stress-Testing: Preparation, Not Prediction

Stress-testing is less glamorous than strategy design and far more uncomfortable. It lives in the shadows, quietly asking the hard questions no one wants to face. What happens if prices start moving three times faster than normal? What if buying and selling suddenly becomes expensive because the gap between what buyers will pay and what sellers want has widened? What if two things that usually move together suddenly move in opposite directions? What if the cost of borrowing money to hold your position jumps in a single day? What if a market you trade in opens far above or below yesterday's closing price?

Stress tests are practice drills. They show you how your strategy behaves at the edges, when the calm, steady conditions you built it for are replaced by noise, scarcity, and surprise. The desks that run these drills regularly tend to last longer. They have already pictured what failure looks like, so when the pressure comes, they are faster to act.

Psychology Alters the Playing Field

Here's the thing about quant's love affair with data: it's missing the most important ingredient. You can have all the historical prices you want, terabytes of tick data going back decades, but nowhere in those spreadsheets will you find a column labeled "human stupidity" or "pants-wetting terror."

The quants build these gorgeous models, fed on years of market data, and they work beautifully—right up until they don't. Because when the real world intrudes, when markets start doing that thing they do where everything goes sideways at once, suddenly all those perfectly calibrated algorithms are trying to predict the behavior of a bunch of primates in expensive suits who are absolutely losing their minds.

Picture this: It's 2 AM, and some trader in London just got a call that makes his blood pressure spike twenty points. He's staring at his screen, and his model is telling him to buy, but his gut is telling him to run. His wife is asking why he's pacing around the kitchen, and his boss is texting him every five minutes. The model doesn't know about the divorce papers he signed last week, or the fact that his biggest client is threatening to pull out, or that he's been surviving on coffee and Adderall for the past three days. So what does he do? He overrides the signal. He cuts his position. He joins the stampede for the exits because, when push comes to shove, humans are still humans, even when they're wearing Bloomberg terminals.

The beautiful irony is that these panic-driven decisions create the very market conditions that make the models even more useless. It's like trying to predict traffic patterns during an earthquake—everyone's driving crazy because everyone else is driving crazy.

In the calm times, sure, people follow their algorithms like good little soldiers. The models hum along nicely, printing money and making everyone feel smart. But when the real action starts—when the phones are ringing and the headlines are screaming and everyone suddenly remembers that they're playing with other people's retirement funds—that's when you find out what your fancy mathematics are really worth. Which is usually not much.

Imperfect by Design

The smartest quants figured this out a long time ago. They build models like pickup trucks—ugly, sturdy, designed to haul manure through a muddy field and keep on going. You want elegant mathematics? Go teach at MIT. You want to make money? Build something that can take a beating.

These guys put big red buttons labeled "STOP" right on their desks. Their systems flash warning lights when correlations start acting funny. They've got manual overrides, circuit breakers, and about seventeen different ways to shut everything down when the computers start behaving like drunk teenagers. Wall Street loves to romanticize the sophisticated algorithms, but the traders making real money year after year are the ones treating their models like suspicious teenagers—never quite trusting them to do the right thing unsupervised.

Markets throw curveballs constantly. Data feeds hiccup at the worst moments. Correlations that held steady for three years suddenly vanish. Some central banker makes an offhand comment on live TV and currencies start spinning like a roulette wheel. The traders who survive expect this chaos. They build their systems paranoid, obsessive, maybe a little crazy—but when markets turn into blenders full of razor blades, these people are still standing at the end of the day, counting profits while everyone else explains to investors why their beautiful equations just exploded.

"The quant who knows when I'm nervous about a position is already halfway to being useful."

Summing Up: Three Pillars, One System

Quant work goes above and beyond the formula itself, and looks everything around it—the data, the assumptions, the infrastructure. Every model depends on the accuracy of its data, and every data feed rests on assumptions about the world. These elements work together as a system—they interact continuously, shaping a system that behaves as more than the sum of its parts. Ignore one, and the other two can't hold. Build with all three in mind, and your tools can remain usable and adaptable.

A quant desk once learned this the hard way. Their model miscalculated the bond's optionality[3] (model), a stale feed inflated the hedge ratio (data), and everyone assumed short-term funding would always be available (assumption). When repo financing[4] dried up in a single afternoon, the position unraveled in days. The math was sound in isolation, the data error looked small, and the funding assumption seemed safe—until all three broke at once.

[3] Bond's optionality means the built-in choices a bond may have—like letting it be turned into stock or paid back early—which can change its value.

[4] Repo financing is a short-term loan where one party sells a security and agrees to buy it back later at a slightly higher price. It's a common way for trading desks to borrow cash using their securities as collateral.

3 Stochastic Wizardry

What They Didn't Teach You in School

Before they learn how to price options or code a mean-reverting strategy, every quant must learn to bow before randomness. Prices zig when they should zag, volatility surges without warning, and the same news causes panic one day and euphoria the next. Finance runs on uncertainty, not certainty, and its equations wear the scars of compromise.

In physics, the elegance of a differential equation reveals truths that persist across time and space. In finance, the elegance of an equation is a comforting lie. Markets move with tension and texture—they flinch, hesitate, and lurch in response to pressure, uncertainty, and emotion. And yet, quants reach for stochastic calculus the way a sailor reaches for stars because it is the only thing pointing toward anything resembling direction.

The Allure and Limits of Brownian Motion

The textbook model of asset price movement, Geometric Brownian Motion (GBM), has an irresistible charm. (Hull, 2012) It's mathematically tractable, analytically elegant, and underpins the Black-Scholes formula that launched a thousand quant careers. In differential form, GBM describes the evolution of a stock price s_t as:

$$ds_t = rs_t\,dt + \sigma s_t\,dW_t$$

Here, r represents the expected rate of return over time. σ encodes volatility—the magnitude of fluctuations around that trend. And dW_t is a Wiener process, a continuous-time stochastic term that captures pure, memoryless randomness. The model assumes that prices move continuously and smoothly through infinitesimal changes.[5]

Figure 3.1a shows what one path of GBM would look like.

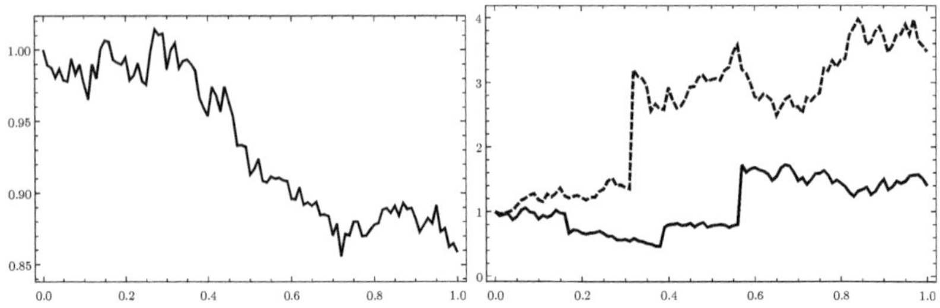

(a) Single Path of GBM (b) Merton Jump Paths

Figure 3.1: GBM vs. Merton's Jumpy Paths: (a) A path of a GBM process with r = 0.1 and $\sigma = 1.0$. This single GBM path appears as continuous, smooth, and jump-free—unlike anything you'd encounter in real markets. (b) Two sample paths of the Merton jump diffusion model with drift $\mu = 0.2$, volatility $\sigma = 0.7$, and jump intensity $\lambda = 3$. The simulation covers a 1-year horizon with daily time steps ($\Delta t = 0.01$) and shows the two sample trajectories.

In theory, the GBM framework offers both simplicity and solvability. In practice, it's a useful fiction—until it isn't. Real markets rarely behave in infinitesimal increments. Prices gap, liquidity vanishes, and volatility clusters. Brownian motion, by construction, cannot jump. Real asset prices do. Events like the 1987 crash or sudden geopolitical shocks fall outside the structure of GBM—highlighting the model's limits in capturing real-world extremes. Labeling events as a "25-sigma move" under GBM highlights the model's limitations—it reflects a structural blind spot. [1]

To address these limitations, quants began extending the GBM framework. They added jump terms through Poisson processes, invoked Lévy flights [2]to allow for discontinuities, and introduced stochastic volatility models like Heston or SABR to capture volatility's own randomness. These refinements improve realism, but they come with their own fragile scaffolding—assumptions about statistical distributions, continuity, and correlation struc-

[5] The term dt reflects a very small time increment—think milliseconds to days, depending on context.

tures. Ironically, these assumptions tend to fail when the market becomes most unpredictable—precisely when the model's guidance is needed most.

So while GBM remains a foundational tool in quantitative finance, its value lies more in its role as a "baseline abstraction" than as a faithful representation of market dynamics. And any quant who treats it as the latter does so at their peril.

When Smooth Stops Working

Stochastic calculus gave quants a language for modeling randomness, albeit an incomplete one. (Hull, 2012) Brownian motion, elegant as it is, implies that markets move continuously—that asset prices evolve in tiny, smooth increments. But real markets lurch. They react to earnings surprises, macroeconomic shocks, and geopolitical events. Prices can go from calm to chaos in a heartbeat.

The intuition is simple, but powerful: most days, asset prices behave like a random walk. But now and then, the market flinches. Merton's model lets you bake that flinch into the math. (Merton, 1976) Each jump is drawn from a probabilistic distribution—often normal or log-normal—and occurs according to a Poisson clock. The result is a process that retains the analytical convenience of Brownian motion, while admitting the messiness of financial reality.

Plotting a few simulated paths under Merton's model reveals the contrast immediately. Instead of the unbroken smoothness of GBM, the paths stutter. Some surge. Others plunge. The baseline randomness remains, but it's been punctuated—disrupted—by moments of discontinuity. And that's what makes it feel more honest. Merton's framework offers no timing for the jumps, merely the structural capacity to account for them.

Of course, this realism comes at a cost. The model's elegance gives way to complexity. Calibration becomes harder. Estimating jump frequency and size requires far more data than most assets can provide. And just like GBM, Merton's model carries assumptions—about independence, jump distributions, and market liquidity—that may themselves break under pressure. Above all, even the jump-extended models can't fully replicate observed market behavior.

Still, it's a meaningful step—one that expands on simpler models by acknowledging a key truth: markets move with friction, jumps, and noise. They rupture. And any quant who recognizes that rupture gains an edge—equipping their model to withstand the shock, the next jump, and for the moment the market truly tests the model.

Merton's Math

The Merton Jump Diffusion Model describes the evolution of a financial asset price s(t) as a stochastic process that integrates both continuous and discontinuous sources of randomness. Formally, the model assumes that the logarithm of the asset price follows a process composed of a Brownian motion and a compound Poisson jump component. The asset price at time t is given by

$$s(t) = s(0) \cdot \exp\left[\left(\mu - \frac{1}{2}\sigma^2 - \lambda\kappa\right)t + \sigma W_t + \sum_{i=1}^{N_t} Y_i\right],$$

where s(0) is the initial price, μ is the drift rate, σ is the volatility of the diffusion component, and W_t is a standard Brownian motion representing continuous market fluctuations. The jump component is governed by a Poisson process N_t with intensity λ, modeling the random arrival of jump events. Each jump has a logarithmic size Y_i, which is drawn from an independent and identically distributed normal distribution with mean μ_J and variance σ_J^2. The term $\kappa = \mathbb{E}[e^{Y_i} - 1]$ represents the expected relative jump size and is used to adjust the drift in order to maintain the martingale property of the price process.

Discrete-Time Recursive Version. In practical applications, Merton's model is implemented in a discrete-time framework. In this setting, the asset price s(t) at discrete time step t can be expressed recursively in terms of its value at the previous time step s(t – 1). Assuming a fixed time increment Δt, the recursive update equation takes the form

$$s(t) = s(t-1) \cdot \exp\left[\left(\mu - \frac{1}{2}\sigma^2 - \lambda\kappa\right)\Delta t + \sigma\sqrt{\Delta t} \cdot Z_t + \sum_{i=1}^{N_t} Y_i\right]$$

where μ is the drift rate, σ is the diffusion volatility, and λ is the intensity of the Poisson jump process. The variable Z_t is a standard normal random variable, $Z_t \sim \mathcal{N}(0, 1)$, representing the Brownian shock over the interval Δt. The term N_t is a Poisson-distributed random variable with mean $\lambda\Delta t$, denoting the number of jumps that occur during the time step. Each jump has a logarithmic size Y_i, which is independently drawn from a normal distribution $\mathcal{N}(\mu_J, \sigma_J^2)$. The total contribution of the jumps within the interval is thus the sum $\sum_{i=1}^{N_t} Y_i$. The parameter $\kappa = \mathbb{E}[e^Y - 1]$, where $Y \sim \mathcal{N}(\mu_J, \sigma_J^2)$, represents the expected relative jump size and is used to adjust the drift for consistency with the continuous-time model.

Meet Kou

The Kou model starts with a simple idea: asset prices don't just drift and wiggle. Sometimes they jump. And those jumps don't always look the same going up as they do going down. Therefore Kou adds asymmetric jump terms to the usual GBM.

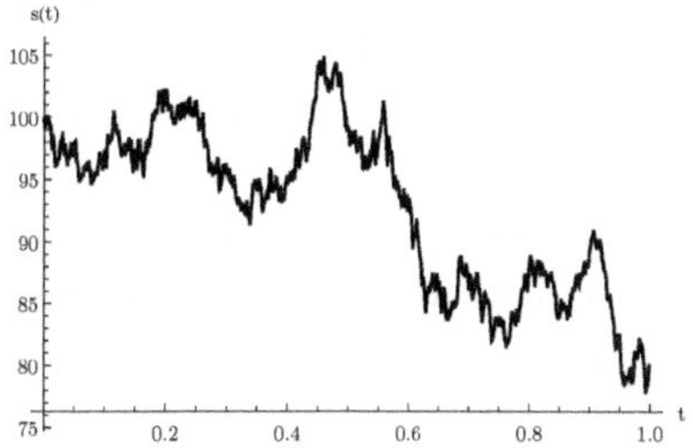

(a) Single Path of Kou's Model

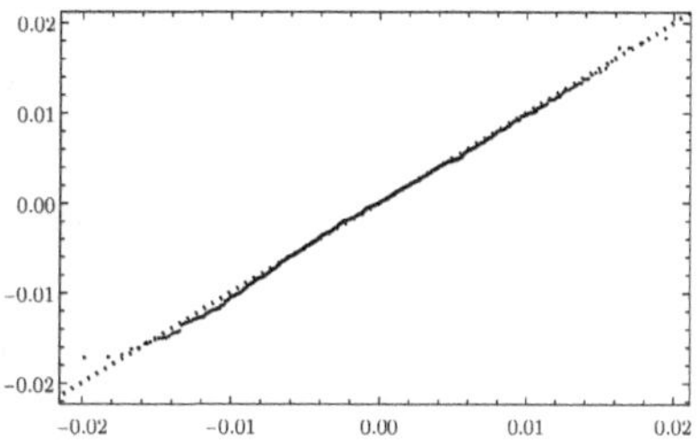

(b) QQ Plot of Kou's Path

Figure 3.2: The Kou Model: (a) Simulated path of the Kou jump-diffusion model with parameters: $s_0 = 100$, $\mu = 0.05$, $\sigma = 0.2$, $\lambda = 0.1$, $p = 0.5$, $\eta_1 = 0.1$, $\eta_2 = 0.1$, $T = 1$, $n = 1000$, $\Delta t = 0.001$. (b) QQ plot of log returns simulated from the Kou jump-diffusion model, with excess kurtosis $k_e = -0.061968$.

In discrete time, the asset price gets updated at each step $t_{i+1} = t_i + \Delta t$ like this:

$$s(t_{i+1}) = s(t_i) \cdot (1 + \mu\Delta t + \sigma\Delta W_i + J_i)\,.$$

The three terms here each do a job:

- $\mu\Delta t$ is drift. It moves prices up (or down) slowly over time.
- $\sigma\Delta W_i$ is noise. A normal shock with variance Δt, drawn from $\mathcal{N}(0, \Delta t)$.
- J_i is the jump. This is where Kou changes the game.

Unlike the Brownian part, J_i is discontinuous. Most of the time it's zero. But with probability $\lambda\Delta t$, a jump happens. That jump size Y_i follows an asymmetric double-exponential distribution:

$$Y_i = \begin{cases} \mathrm{Exp}(\eta_1), & \text{with probability } p, \\ -\mathrm{Exp}(\eta_2), & \text{with probability } 1 - p. \end{cases}$$

So big upward jumps are rare but possible, while sharp downward crashes are more likely. In full:

$$J_i = \begin{cases} Y_i, & \text{with probability } \lambda\Delta t, \\ 0, & \text{otherwise.} \end{cases}$$

That's it. The brilliance is in the asymmetry. By letting jumps be sudden, skewed, and heavy-tailed, Kou's model does something Black-Scholes can't: it mimics the messiness of real financial markets—where crashes are fast and booms are slow.

In effect, Kou's model takes Merton's idea and gives it street sense. His jump sizes follow a double exponential distribution—meaning large downward moves are more likely than big upward ones. [3]

Kou vs. Merton

To see the difference between Merton and Kou's jump models, you could simulate 1000 jump events under each. In Merton's world, jumps are drawn from a normal distribution with 0% mean and 5% standard deviation. As expected, the results fell within a symmetric range of approximately ±15%—clean, orderly, and statistically neutral.

Kou's model is designed with a strong, deliberate tilt toward downside realism—reflecting the way risk actually shows up in markets. Using the double exponential distribution, we assigned 70% of jumps to be downward and larger in magnitude, while upward jumps occurred just 30% of the time and were typically smaller. The simulation matched intuition: nearly 70% of Kou jumps breached −10%, while only 30% crept past +10%—a sharp asymmetry that Merton would miss entirely (see Figure 3.3).

One trader described using Merton in a high-volatility regime as "driving with your headlights on, but only in fog where every turn's a coin toss." Another said switching to Kou "was like finally admitting gravity works."

The contrast is sharp. Merton's model gives you balance; Kou's gives you realism. And when you're managing real risk—not just pricing it—the difference matters. A model that treats all jumps equally may be mathematically fair but practically naïve.

If you're managing risk on a quiet day, Merton's model works fine. But if you're holding a book through earnings season or trading options around a geopolitical headline, Kou's asymmetric jump structure better captures the feel of the market—nervous, one-sided, and just a little unfair.

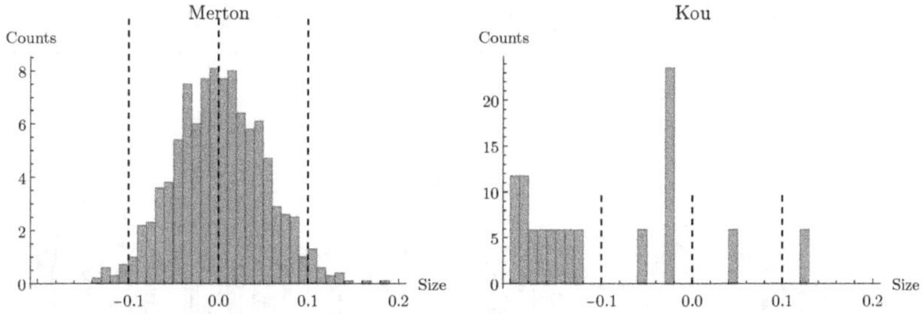

Figure 3.3: Empirical distributions of simulated jump sizes under Merton's normal model (left) and Kou's double exponential model (right). The vertical dashed lines at ±10% highlight how frequently large downside moves occur under Kou's asymmetric structure.

Because in real markets, jumps aren't neutral. They tend to lean and slant and gravitate. And models that ignore this propensity, give risk a nice, clean mask.

Long Tails: Where the Monsters Live

Assuming normally distributed returns gives a false sense of control. The standard normal has thin tails. Financial returns do not. The empirical distributions are leptokurtic—meaning longer tails and more frequent extremes. What should be a once-a-century event happens every few years.

To see what long tails really imply, turn to Figure 3.4, which compares two distinct asset classes: gold and the S&P500—Wall Street's benchmark barometer.

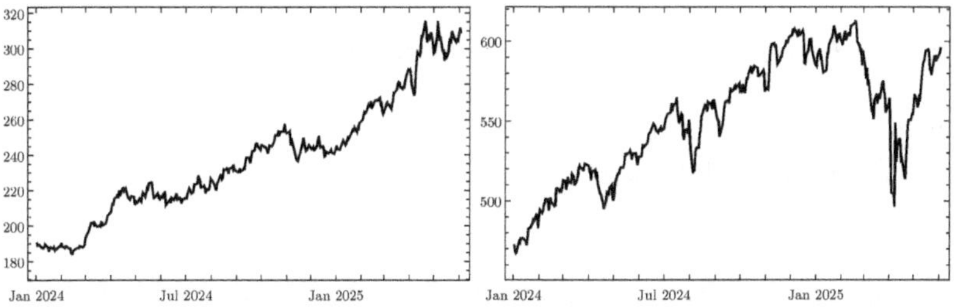

(a) SPDR Gold Trust

(b) SPDR S&P500 ETF Trust

Figure 3.4: Two well-known securities: Gold and the S&P500 Index

Their log returns (in %) are shown in Figure 3.5. At first glance, they resemble noise—random fluctuations with the occasional spike—offering little visual hint of what lies beneath.

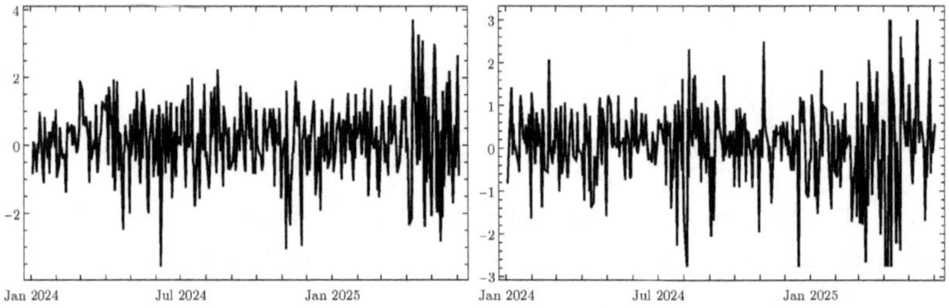

(a) Log returns of Gold Trus (b) Log returns of S&P500 ETF Trust

Figure 3.5: Snapshots of the log returns of two well-known securities: Gold and the S&P500 Index

However, the histograms of the two log returns help in Figure 3.6 to unravel the differences.

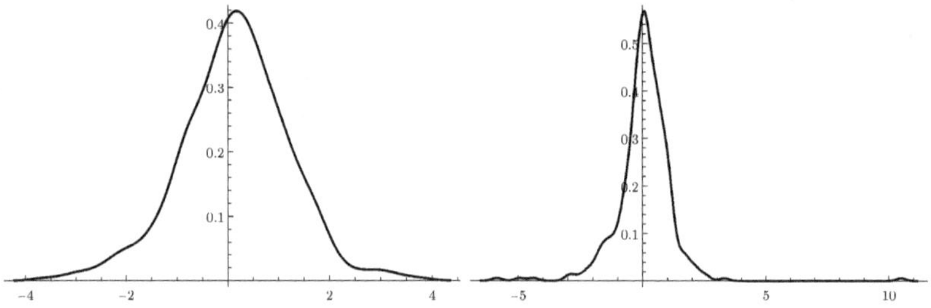

(a) Histogram of log returns of Gold Trus (b) Histogram of log returns of S&P500

Figure 3.6: Histograms of the log returns of two well-known securities: Gold and the S&P500 Index

To see just how far reality can stray from theory, take a look at the QQ plots in Figure 3.7.

Deviations tell a different story: skewed data curves away—upward for right-skew, downward for left—while heavy tails lift the ends of the plot above the line and light tails pull them below. In short, the closer the dots cling to that line, the safer it is to assume normality.

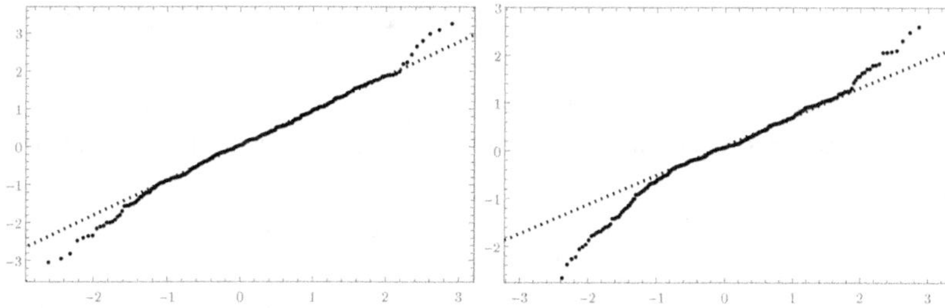

(a) QQ of log returns of Gold Trus (b) QQ of log returns of S&P500

Figure 3.7: QQ plots help to visualize the long tails: note the upward and downward deviations in the tails where extreme returns occur more often than the Gaussian benchmark would predict.

If returns truly followed a normal distribution, the points would align along the diagonal. But they don't. The center may match, but the tails always betray the truth—real markets are full of monsters.

Some firms still cling to Gaussian assumptions, using Value-at-Risk (VaR) metrics based on standard deviation. Others try to patch the hole using t-distributions, extreme value theory, or generalized Pareto fits. But fitting the tails is never clean. There's not enough data. And the tails, by their nature, are the parts of the distribution we see the least—until they eat us alive.

Kurtosis: Quantifying the Monsters

The QQ plots make the story visual—but it's backed by numbers too. One of the most telling metrics is excess kurtosis, a statistical measure of how heavy the tails of a distribution are compared to the normal.

In a standard normal distribution, the kurtosis is 3. Excess kurtosis is defined as the kurtosis of the distribution minus 3:

$$\kappa_e = \frac{1}{n}\sum_{i=1}^{n}\left(\frac{x_i - \bar{x}}{s}\right)^4 - 3$$

where x_i are the individual returns, $\bar{x}$ is the sample mean, s is the sample standard deviation, and n is the number of observations.

In this formulation a value of 0 means the distribution has the same tail weight as a normal distribution, a positive value indicates fat tails—more frequent extreme deviations, and a negative value (rare in finance) would suggest thin tails—fewer outliers.

For example, if the excess kurtosis of GLD returns is 0.826128, and that of the S&P500 is 21.5686, both values reveal leptokurtic behavior—more prone to extreme outcomes than the bell curve implies. The S&P500 might spike or crash more violently; GLD might exhibit persistent tail events during volatility shocks.

Unlike volatility, which describes the spread of returns, kurtosis speaks to their shape. It provides a numerical lens that confirms what QQ plots already show: markets carry extreme noise—volatility and shocks that exceed the limits of Gaussian models.

"The model assumes volatility is constant. The market disagrees."

The Practical Quant's Checklist

Begin with a model, because without one, you're flying blind. But don't fall in love with it. Every model, no matter how elegant, rests on assumptions that break down when the environment shifts. Maybe it assumes liquidity that vanishes under stress, or stable correlations that snap the moment fear enters the market. If you trust the model too much, you're not using it—you're worshipping it.

Build with long tails in mind. Markets don't move like textbooks suggest. They jump, lurch, and cascade. Distributions that assume normality underestimate the frequency and severity of real-world shocks. Treat anything that ignores fat tails as a liability—because when the improbable happens, it tends to happen fast, and it tends to be expensive.

Volatility isn't a static input—it's a living, shifting variable. It behaves differently in bull markets, bear markets, and flash crashes. So don't just model it as time-varying. Recognize that it changes character across regimes. A strategy that survives calm won't necessarily survive a storm.

Stress-testing is mandatory. You might build a model that doesn't account for jumps—maybe because it's mathematically convenient or computationally efficient. But your portfolio doesn't care about that. It will be exposed to jump risk whether your code includes it or not. So simulate shocks. Force your strategy to live through panics, liquidity crunches, and correlated selloffs—even if only on paper. It's the only way to see where things will tear.

Above all, use mathematics to give your system structure, not to pretend that you've captured truth. The market rewards models that hold up under pressure—models that stay reliable, adaptable, and functional under real-world stress. Robustness beats elegance. A quant's job is to stay standing when the unexpected hits and when others are caught off guard.

Tools Are Not Shields

Stochastic models gave quants a language for describing randomness. But the market speaks in dialects the textbooks never teach. It murmurs in autocorrelation, shouts in long tails, and whispers in liquidity fractures. The models help—but only if you watch out for the parts that they miss.

A good quant writes clean SDEs. A great one knows when to stop pretending the SDE is real. Quant tools are necessary, and the smartest quants build around uncertainty instead of trying to eliminate it.

Notes for Chapter 3

1. Financial markets have experienced several high-sigma events—extreme occurrences that traditional models like GBM consider nearly impossible. In 1998, Russia defaulted on its sovereign debt, triggering a chain reaction that led to the collapse of LTCM, where the hedge fund's own models had estimated the resulting market losses as 25-sigma events—supposedly so rare as to be virtually impossible. Yet the event occurred, revealing a critical flaw: even sophisticated, heavily leveraged strategies failed to account for tail risk.

   A decade later, the Global Financial Crisis of 2007–2008 happened. The world witnessed the systemic failure of major financial institutions and a massive collapse in asset values. Some quantitative models described the daily market swings during this period as 10- to 25-sigma events. What were labeled as rare events began to cluster and cascade, revealing a deeper flaw: standard risk models failed concomitantly in their forecasts and in their very assumptions about reality.

2. Lévy flights model movement as a mix of many small steps and occasional large jumps—something standard Brownian motion cannot capture. In GBM, price changes are smooth and extreme moves are highly unlikely. But real markets can shift abruptly due to news, liquidity shocks, or panic.

   Lévy flights allow for such discontinuous, heavy-tailed behavior. As part of the broader class of Lévy processes, they extend Brownian motion by including sudden jumps, better reflecting the fat-tailed nature of asset returns.

   They offer a more realistic kind of randomness—one that accounts not only for everyday fluctuations but also for rare, dramatic shifts that can reshape a portfolio in an instant.

3. Figure 3.2b shows that the distribution of the log returns of Kou's model is quite light-tailed. This is because $\Delta W_i \sim \mathcal{N}(0, \Delta t)$ dominates under the given parameters.

4 Modeling vs. Trading

The Ivory Tower Meets the Bloodbath

A trader once taped a Post-it note to his monitor: "Models don't trade. Traders do." He wasn't mocking quants. He was summarizing an unspoken rule on the floor. The quant's model might be sharper. The trader's screen decides what actually gets done.

This is the friction zone: the point where theoretical elegance meets execution reality. Most quants enter finance believing models will drive decisions. They learn quickly that decisions shape how models get used—or whether they get used at all.

Different Frames, Same Market

Quants come to the market with equations. Traders come with scars. One optimizes; the other improvises.

To a quant, a model that maximizes expected return under a defined risk constraint feels complete—tidy, like a well-packed suitcase. The math checks out. The assumptions are explicit. The Sharpe ratio gleams. But hand that model to a trader, and the first question isn't about parameters or priors. It's: "What happens when this goes illiquid?" Not because the trader distrusts the model. But because she remembers February 5, 2018[6]—or March 2020[7]—or that unremarkable Tuesday when a Turkish bond desk hiccupped and a

[6] *Volmageddon*: Volatility spiked and wiped out short-volatility strategies. See (Augustin et al., 2021).

[7] The COVID-19 panic triggered extreme market stress.

liquidity cascade followed. She's lived the one bad day the model averages away.[8]

The quant runs simulations across a hundred well-behaved days and sees signal. The trader sees the ninety-ninth percentile and wonders who's on the other side of the trade when the spread blows out. The model's confidence is statistical. The trader's skepticism is biological.

A machine learning model might flag a sweet cluster of intraday signals—predictive, precise, elegantly backtested. But the trader knows how that signal feels at 8:31 a.m. when a central bank surprise sucks the liquidity out of the book like oxygen from a room. What's interpreted as resistance in the model might be a spoof. That spike in volume might be panic, not opportunity.

They're not at odds, the quant and the trader. They just live in different time zones. The quant sees patterns. The trader sees exceptions. And the market punishes the one who forgets the other exists.

[8] Most models rely on averages, expected values, or typical scenarios. They smooth out the extremes. But in markets, one bad day—a tail event—can destroy a portfolio. If you've lived through it, you know that averages are not the whole story.

The Model Isn't Wrong—Just Not Enough

Models work. That's not the issue. The issue is they don't work alone.

A model can price risk with surgical elegance—until the operating table starts to shake. Most are built on an implicit assumption that the market structure holds: liquidity aplenty, correlations behave, execution is frictionless. That assumption holds under certain conditions—but it's sensitive and requires careful handling. And like most fragile things, you only notice it after it breaks.

In quiet markets, a pairs trade mean-reverts like clockwork. In a stress regime, the clock melts. Correlations that looked stable for five years evaporate in five minutes. The ETF that tracked the index suddenly doesn't. The hedge that was supposed to reduce exposure instead magnifies it.

It's not about the math being flawed. The curve-fitting, the backtesting, the statistical rigor—they're all done correctly. What's missing is what doesn't fit on a spreadsheet: the context, the crowding, the market's mood.The risk lies in overreliance—believing the model captures the full picture, when it's only one perspective in a larger, more complex environment.

When too many desks run the same strategy off the same historical signals, the exits get jammed. Everyone's calibrated to yesterday's truth. But markets don't send calendar invites before regime changes. They just move. And when they do, the model stays still.

This affirms the value of modeling—while grounding it in the reality of its limits and context. Models are necessary. They're just not sufficient.

Execution: Where Clean Models Get Dirty

On paper, execution looks easy. In practice, it's where clean models get muddy.

Backtests are tidy by nature. They assume you can slip in and out of positions without touching the water—no slippage, no impact, no footprints. But real markets are less like spreadsheets and more like crowded hallways: move too quickly, and you shove someone; move too slowly, and you miss the exit.

A strong signal doesn't mean a strong return—not if you're trying to act on it through a keyhole of liquidity. You can model the alpha, but if you can't capture it without moving the price, it's not real. It's theoretical profit in a world that doesn't trade theoretically.

Execution is the bottleneck that turns ideal trades into practical compromises. A model might declare, with mathematical confidence: "Buy 40,000 shares at the mid." That's cute. It doesn't ask what happens when you hit the first 10,000 and the rest of the market sees you coming. The mid doesn't wait politely—it moves.

This is where market microstructure stops being an elective and becomes essential. Order types, venue selection, and timing strategies won't appear in a model's Sharpe ratio—but they quietly determine whether that Sharpe is actionable or imaginary.

Models like Almgren–Chriss were built to confront this exact tension: the trade-off between market impact and execution risk. (Almgren and Chriss, 2001)

$$C(x) = \lambda x + \eta x^2$$

Here, x is trade size, λ captures linear impact (like spread), and η captures nonlinear slippage from market depth.

Example 4.1. Cost of Trade Execution. Suppose a trader plans to execute a block trade with the following parameters:

$\lambda = 0.01$	linear cost per unit, e.g., from bid-ask spread
$\eta = 0.005$	nonlinear cost coefficient, e.g., due to market depth
Trade sizes	$x \in \{100, 500, 1000\}$

Table 4.1: When Size Starts to Hurt: Nonlinear Execution Costs

x	$\lambda x + \eta x^2$	C(x)
100	$0.01 \times 100 + 0.005 \times 100^2$	51
500	$0.01 \times 500 + 0.005 \times 500^2$	1256
1000	$0.01 \times 1000 + 0.005 \times 1000^2$	5010

The linear term in the second column of Table 4.1 grows proportionally with trade size—it's the steady, predictable cost, like paying the toll every time you cross a bridge. But the quadratic term scales much faster. As trade size increases, it dominates the total cost. This captures a core truth of market execution: costs don't just rise with size—they accelerate, especially when your order starts to lean on the edge of liquidity.

In practice, this means a small trade might go unnoticed, but a large block can ripple through the order book, moving prices and triggering defensive algorithms on the other side. Execution costs reflect both your intentions and the market's response—shaped by your actions and the ripple effects they create. □

Traders liked the Almgren–Chriss model—until they tried using it during earnings season. (Almgren and Chriss, 2001) On paper, it elegantly balances market impact against timing risk, carving out an "optimal" execution path across time slices. In practice, the model assumes the market doesn't flinch when you show your hand. One buy-side desk would find that the model's trajectory looked brilliant in backtests—other market players began to anticipate and trade ahead of their orders, pushing prices against them. Competitors sniffed out the pattern and started stepping in ahead of the scheduled trades. The lesson wasn't that Almgren–Chriss was inappropriate—it was that its assumptions were public, and markets adapt. Execution shows what you're doing. Do it enough, and the market starts guessing what you'll do next.

Quants who understand this asymmetry design more resilient strategies. They know that models don't operate in a vacuum—they operate downstream from execution constraints. And when those constraints are ignored, even the sharpest alpha can get lost in the slippage.

Speed Wins Different Games

In HFT, the objective is speed—executing actions faster than the competition to gain an edge. Nanoseconds matter more than insight. Hardware wins.

HFT firms use models, but performance depends on latency. The Avellaneda–Stoikov framework, used in market-making, shows how inventory risk influences quotes:

$$q^*(t) = -\frac{\theta}{\gamma\sigma^2}(p - S_t)$$

Example 4.2. Optimal Quote with Inventory Pressure. Consider a high-frequency market maker operating under the Avellaneda–Stoikov framework. Let the parameters be:

$\theta = 1.0$	inventory level (positive for long position)
$\gamma = 0.05$	risk aversion coefficient
$\sigma = 2.0$	volatility of the asset
$S_t = 100.00$	current mid-price
$p = 100.50$	reference price (e.g., expected future price)

Using the formula:

$$q^*(t) = -\frac{\theta}{\gamma\sigma^2}(p - S_t)$$

now plug in the values:

$$q^*(t) = -\frac{1.0}{0.05 \times 2.0^2}(100.50 - 100.00) = -\frac{1.0}{0.2}(0.50) = -2.5$$

A computed quote skew of $q^*(t) = -2.5$ tells us something simple: the market maker wants to reduce inventory. That value doesn't signal where prices are headed; it just tilts the quotes to encourage more selling than buying. If the inventory is too high, the system nudges quotes to slow down incoming buy orders and speed up the sell-side. The goal is to let the market help rebalance the position, one trade at a time.

This happens at speeds measured in microseconds. Human intuition isn't fast enough to do this manually, which is why the logic sits inside an algorithm. The decision-making process focuses on rapid response—adjusting to positions and flows quickly enough to maintain solvency and seize opportunity. □

The Avellaneda–Stoikov framework is built for this kind of environment. It's not designed to forecast markets in the traditional sense. Instead, it provides a set of rules for quoting prices in real time while accounting for inventory pressure and market activity. In high-frequency trading, the advantage usually comes from getting to the queue first, not from having the most elaborate view on where the market might go.

Quote decisions in this setting aren't opinions about direction. They're short-lived responses to imbalances, constrained by inventory and shaped by latency. Speed matters. Execution logic matters. Everything else is just extra.

Traders Don't Disregard Models—They Filter Them

A quant might hand over an optimized portfolio. A trader might pare it back—cutting the exposure to a small-cap stock with limited float, swapping out an illiquid ETF, or reducing leverage on a risk cluster that looks benign on paper but feels radioactive in the market. This is interpretation—an active effort to understand, frame, and respond with clarity.

Models abstract. Traders compress abstractions into executables. What looks optimal in the model may be impractical, or even dangerous, at the point of trade. A portfolio may assume instantaneous fills or ignore execution costs that balloon in volatile regimes. A trader, sitting on a live order book, knows that *printing a block*[9] in a *thin name*[10] is tantamount to moving the market against yourself. This means that a trader, who can see the actual live market depth (the order book), understands that trying to execute a large trade in an illiquid stock will likely push the price unfavorably — you'll pay more to buy, or receive less when selling, simply because your own order is moving the market.

Traders use inputs the model doesn't see: incoming order flow, hidden liquidity, desk flows, timing games around macro announcements. A risk-off tilt may be dialed up an hour before a Fed decision. A statistically attractive cross-sector pair may be shelved because it cuts across two desks with conflicting mandates. A low-volatility long might be dropped not for its stats, but for its lack of narrative—the market simply isn't buying that story this week.

The most useful models are interpretable, not just accurate. They surface drivers, highlight sensitivities, and expose assumptions. They tell you why—not just what. And the most effective quants build with judgment in mind. They don't lock the trader into a fixed output—they create scaffolds that hold up under real-world pressure.

A model that says "buy" is fine. A model that says "buy, but here's why, and here's where it breaks" is better. Because in the end, the trader doesn't blindly follow. They filter, weigh, and override—guided not just by math, but by what the market is whispering between the ticks.

[9] Slang for executing a large order (a "block trade") — often several times larger than typical trade sizes in that asset.

[10] A stock or security with low liquidity — meaning it trades infrequently, has a wide bid-ask spread, or small volume at each price level in the order book.

"Your model is elegant. My button moves $50 million."

How Quants Work Inside Trading Teams

Quants on trading desks operate in a different rhythm than their counterparts in research. Their work is built for real-time friction. Code must run cleanly under pressure. Logic must hold when prices move fast. And explanations must land in seconds, because the questions will come mid-trade, not in a review session.

They don't chase micro-optimizations. Instead, they prepare for real-world strain—market halts, volatility spikes, network lags. Resilience matters more than refinement. A model that fails gracefully is more valuable than one that excels in ideal conditions. Desk quants wire in fallbacks, sanity checks, and logs that actually get read.

Communication is as much a tool as code. A model's utility depends on how well its purpose is understood. On the desk, even smart ideas fail if they sound like puzzles. It's not about simplifying the math—it's about matching the mental model of the person making the trade. "The LSTM flags hidden regimes" becomes "it picks up when short-term flow reverses." The former explains the architecture. The latter connects to action.

A desk quant once built a PCA-based anomaly detector[11] for sector flows. Initially, it went unused—too abstract. He reframed the output as a "sneaky exits" signal, showing when certain names were being quietly unwound. After that, traders started checking it daily. The math didn't change, but the framing did.

Successful models are fully integrated—they feed into dashboards, support pre-trade checks, and guide execution. They function as active participants in decision-making, shaping outcomes in real time. The same applies to the quant. Lasting impact comes from embedding into the team's rhythm—knowing what trades matter, when risk feels different, and where tools need to bend.

One PM put it clearly: "The quant who knows when I'm nervous about a position is already halfway to being useful." It's about staying close to the trade—anchored in real market dynamics, where theory meets execution.

Where Code Meets the Trade

Modeling and trading operate under different pressures, timelines, and incentives. The model abstracts a world into equations and code. The trade responds to what the world actually does—often with urgency. Both sides aim at the same goal, but they speak in different dialects.

Quants who thrive inside this tension do more than build clean models. They build trust. That means stress-testing ideas in messy environments, translating abstract signals into trader-relevant language, and revisiting assumptions after every misfire. They don't disappear after deployment. They stay close to the action, refining outputs as new data and desk feedback roll in.

A model that generates good results in backtests isn't enough. It must remain stable when the market gaps, and it must degrade gracefully under data loss or latency. Traders want tools they can use in real time—clear, actionable, and built for moments when time is short and consequences are immediate.

The quants who endure learn the rhythm of real-world trading. They watch how their models behave not just in theory, but in practice—under volatility spikes, news-driven flows, or sudden liquidity drops. They track which

[11] A PCA-based anomaly detector uses Principal Component Analysis to learn the typical patterns in how data (like stock prices or sector flows) move together. When new data deviates significantly from these established patterns, it flags the behavior as unusual. In trading, this helps surface hidden activity—like a quiet exit from a position—by spotting moves that don't align with the usual market rhythm.

signals get acted on and which ones get quietly ignored. That feedback loop becomes part of their design process.

In the end, the models that last are interpretable, actionable, and resilient. They are built for trust under pressure—designed to hold up when markets turn chaotic, with reliability prioritized over elegance. Likewise, the quants who last are clear in their communication, collaborative under pressure, and relentless about testing their assumptions in live fire.

A strategy that works on paper is a start. A strategy that traders actually use—under pressure, at scale, in real portfolios—is the one that matters.

5 Risk

The Four-Letter Word That Runs the World

"To measure is to know. If you cannot measure it, you cannot improve it."

—William Thomson, Lord Kelvin

"Using volatility as a measure of risk is nuts. Risk to us is 1) the risk of permanent loss of capital, or 2) the risk of inadequate return."

—Charlie Munger

Risk is the invisible force that governs financial markets. (Hull, 2023) Every trade, every investment, and every model is an attempt to quantify, control, or exploit risk. Yet, despite its omnipresence, risk remains one of the least understood concepts in finance. Some treat it as an abstract mathematical construct, reducing it to volatility measures and statistical distributions. Others see it as an unavoidable part of human behavior, a psychological game of fear and greed. Both perspectives are necessary, yet neither is sufficient.

Risk is neither fully measurable nor entirely controllable. At best, it can be "estimated" and managed. At worst, it is ignored until it manifests in catastrophic losses. From the collapse of LTCM in 1998 to the 2008 financial crisis and countless blowups in between, the history of finance is a story of underestimated risk. The question every quant must answer is whether their model can withstand being wrong—built to survive, adapt, and recover under real-world stress.

"Risk is when you don't know what you're doing."

The Many Faces of Risk

Market risk gets the spotlight. It's what people imagine when they think of volatility—prices moving up or down, sometimes violently. But that's just one layer.

Liquidity risk matters just as much. It's the risk that a position can't be exited at the expected price. This isn't hypothetical. In 2007, funds holding similar strategies tried to unwind positions at once. Prices gapped. What should have been manageable losses turned into career-ending blows.

Credit risk works differently. It's about counterparty risk—whether the other side meets its obligations, regardless of price movement. The Gaussian copula model gave an illusion of safety by assuming stable correlations between credit events. In 2008, that illusion broke. The defaults clustered. The math didn't help.

Operational risk is more invisible. Bugs in code, bad data feeds, misconfigured risk engines—these don't come with price charts. But they cause just as much damage. Knight Capital lost $440 million in 45 minutes because an old code module activated during a deployment. The market didn't move against them. Their system moved against itself.

Rare Events Happen Often

The normal distribution suggests that large deviations are improbable. Markets say otherwise.

Crashes like Black Monday in 1987, the Russian default in 1998, the 2008 financial crisis, and the pandemic-driven selloff in 2020 all occurred more often than their modeled probabilities would suggest. Each one had been labeled a once-in-a-century event by someone's model. Most happened within two decades of each other.

Black Monday alone—October 19, 1987—saw the Dow plunge over 22% in a single day. Under a normal distribution, that was a 30-sigma event—mathematically impossible, if the model were right. But it happened, and it happened fast. The cause went above and beyond macro fear—it was portfolio insurance strategies feeding on themselves, mechanically selling as prices fell. The models missed the reflexivity. They assumed the market was a passive environment—one that absorbs trades but doesn't react to them. But on Black Monday, the system fed on itself. Portfolio insurance strategies, designed to sell as prices dropped, created a feedback loop: falling prices triggered more selling, which pushed prices down further, which in turn triggered even more selling. The models treated each trade as independent. The market didn't. It became a self-reinforcing chain reaction—reflexivity in action.

In 1998, Long-Term Capital Management collapsed after the Russian government defaulted on its debt. LTCM was staffed by Nobel laureates and armed with elegant models, yet it folded under a crisis that was "un-hedgeable" by design. Liquidity dried up, spreads exploded, and correlations that were supposed to stay low surged instead. The tails didn't just wag the dog—they ate it.

Then came 2008. AAA-rated mortgage-backed securities, modeled as near risk-free, imploded in a cascade of credit failures. Institutions that relied on Gaussian copulas[12] to manage portfolio risk found themselves marking down assets that had no buyers. Correlation estimates broke. Funding markets froze. VaR models that assumed diversification would protect against large losses failed when every asset started moving together.

[12] A Gaussian copula is a model that links individual risks together by assuming their dependencies follow a normal pattern. It was widely used to price complex credit products—until those assumptions failed during the 2008 crisis.

Even the 2020 pandemic crash, while "exogenous"[13] in origin, exposed the same modeling weakness: assumptions of smooth adaptation. In March, markets went from complacent to frozen in a matter of days. Bid-ask spreads widened, circuit breakers triggered, and once again, events expected once a century emerged within a few short years—reminding markets how frequently the extreme can show up.

Figure 5.1 traces the DJIA across four historical crash events. These are market ruptures that models were never built to handle. The charts show the sharp discontinuity on Black Monday in 1987, the cascading volatility during the 2008 crisis, and the sudden COVID drop in 2020. The frequency and severity of these drawdowns visually reinforce what the math missed: extreme events don't wait a hundred years. Sometimes they cluster. Sometimes they come in threes.

Even with different causes, each episode shares one trait: the assumptions behind "normal" broke down exactly when they were most needed.

Each crisis was different in cause, but similar in what it revealed. Models underestimated the tails and mischaracterized the market's dynamics. Feedback loops, leverage, liquidity evaporation—all factors too nonlinear, too human, to fit neatly into a normal distribution.

Maximum Drawdown: Measuring Financial Pain

In the study of financial risk, MDD stands apart as a measure that captures something most models ignore: the psychological and practical pain of *staying invested through a loss.* MDD in fact documents what *actually happened*—how far a portfolio fell from its peak before clawing its way back, if it did at all.

To see MDD in action, take a look at figure 5.2.

Notice a peak (marked by •) sometime in early August 1987, followed by a trough (marked by ⊗) in October of the same year. Also note that the DJIA never recovered back to the peak in 1987. Table 5.1 shows what you expect the MDD calculation to provide.

[13] In finance, an *exogenous* shock is an event that originates outside the market or model—something the system doesn't cause or anticipate internally. The COVID-19 pandemic was exogenous because it began as a public health crisis but triggered widespread financial disruption.

(a) Derivatives Spirals in 1987

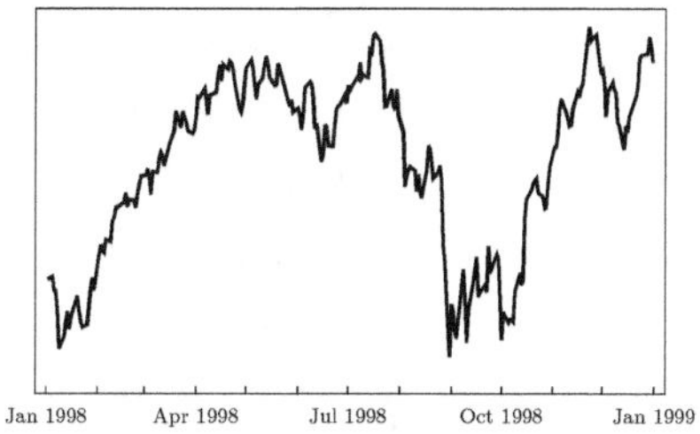

(b) Russian Debt Default 1998

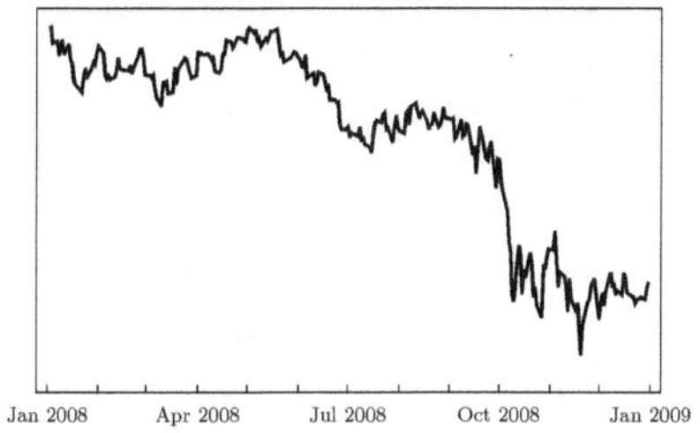

(c) Credit Contagion in 2008

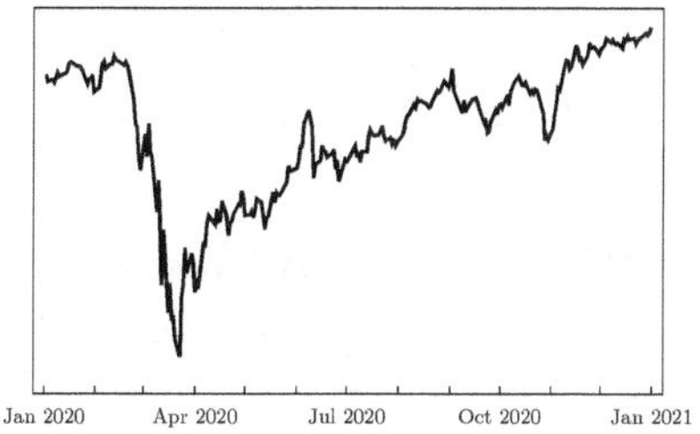

(d) Pandemic Panic in 2020

Figure 5.1: Dow Jones Industrial Average levels during major crash events: 1987, 1998, 2008, and 2020. The scale and speed of these drawdowns highlight the limitations of models assuming normally distributed returns.

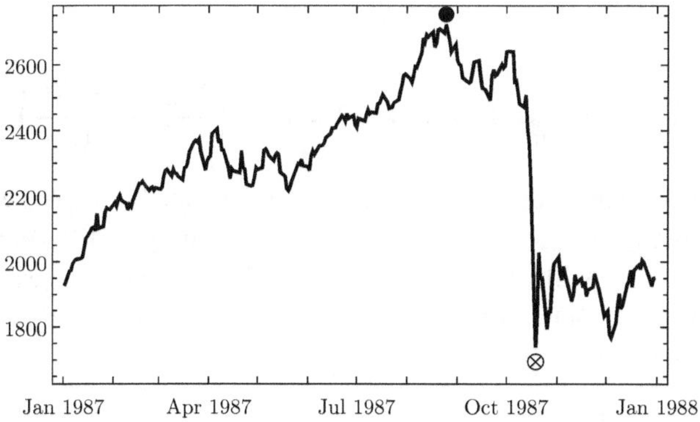

Figure 5.2: Black Monday October 1987: Peak and Trough of DJIA

Metric	Value
Max Drawdown (%)	36.13
Peak Date	Tue 25 Aug 1987
Peak Value	2722.42
Trough Date	Mon 19 Oct 1987
Trough Value	1738.74
Recovery Date	Not Recovered
Drawdown Duration (days)	N/A

Table 5.1: Maximum Drawdown of DJIA for Black Monday 1987

MDD Math Let V(t) denote the value of a portfolio at trading day t, where $t \in [0, T]$. The running peak of the portfolio up to time t is defined as:

$$V_{peak}(t) = \max_{s \leq t} V(s)$$

The drawdown at time t is then the percentage decline from this historical peak:

$$\text{Drawdown}(t) = \frac{V_{peak}(t) - V(t)}{V_{peak}(t)}$$

The maximum drawdown MDD over the interval [0, T] is the largest such drop:

$$\text{MDD} = \max_{t \in [0,T]} \text{Drawdown}(t) = \max_{t \in [0,T]} \left(\frac{V_{peak}(t) - V(t)}{V_{peak}(t)} \right)$$

This is a path-dependent metric. It cares not just about where the portfolio ended up but how it got there. A flat line followed by a 20% drop and immediate recovery will generate the same terminal return as a steady upward march, but the MDD will reveal the temporary devastation the investor had to endure in the first case.

This simple but powerful metric does not rely on any probabilistic model or parametric distribution. It is entirely empirical and speaks to the worst actual loss an investor experienced if they bought at the peak and sold at the bottom. The longer the drawdown lasts, the harder it is—both financially and emotionally—to hold the position. MDD is therefore widely used by fund managers, allocators, and risk officers not just to assess performance but to test psychological fortitude.

Beyond the Threshold: Risk Quantified

VaR is a widely used risk measure that attempts to quantify how extreme a portfolio's losses might be—under "normal" market conditions. It provides a probabilistic boundary on potential losses over a given time horizon. For instance, if a portfolio's one-day VaR at the 95% confidence level is $10 million, it implies the following:

> "There's a 95% chance the portfolio will not lose more than $10 million tomorrow."

This does not mean that losses will never exceed $10 million; rather, it suggests such a daily loss are is to happen at most 5% of the time, under the model's assumptions.

Mathematically, VaR at level $\alpha \in (0, 1)$ is defined as:

$$\mathrm{VaR}_\alpha = -\inf\{x \in \mathbb{R} \mid P(L > x) \leq \alpha\}$$

where L denotes the portfolio loss over a fixed time horizon, and α is the chosen tail probability level.

In practice, VaR_α is often computed as the negative of the α-quantile of the profit-and-loss (P&L) distribution:

$$\mathrm{VaR}_\alpha = -q_\alpha(L),$$

where $q_\alpha(L)$ is the α-quantile:

$$q_\alpha(L) = \inf\{x \in \mathbb{R} \mid P(L \leq x) \geq \alpha\}.$$

This formulation aligns with empirical or simulation-based estimation methods using as historical data.

The minus sign in the definition reflects a convention: since losses are positive by definition ($L > 0$), VaR is reported as a positive number, representing a capital buffer. So, while the quantile q_α may be negative (for example, a large loss in dollar terms), VaR is stated in absolute magnitude.

It is important to note that VaR is a "threshold metric," not a bound on worst-case losses. It tells us nothing about what happens beyond the threshold—the severity or distribution of tail losses. This limitation has prompted the use of complementary risk measures such as CVaR[14] which consider the expected loss in the tail region beyond VaR.

Finally, VaR depends on both the time horizon (e.g., one day vs. ten days) and the confidence level (e.g., 95% vs. 99%), and its reliability hinges on the accuracy of the assumed loss distribution. Under non-normal or heavy-tailed models, such as those incorporating jumps or volatility clustering, conventional VaR methods may significantly underestimate risk.

Hindsight Before Foresight

MDD tells you the worst case of what actually happened.[15] It measures the steepest fall from a portfolio's peak to its lowest trough before a new high was reached. In plain terms: if you had bought at the top and sold at the bottom, what's the most you could've lost? That's your MDD. It's usually quoted as a percentage and doesn't care how quickly or slowly the loss unfolded—just how deep it went.

This is a *realized* loss, not a hypothetical one. No assumptions about volatility or statistical distribution are required. It's entirely based on the portfolio's historical path. If a fund grew to $10 million, dropped to $7 million, then bounced back, the MDD was 30%. It captures the pain of watching value disappear in real time—whether over days or years.

Now contrast that with VaR, which is forward-looking.[16] It tries to quantify how much a portfolio *might* lose over a given time horizon, at a given confidence level. A 95% one-day VaR of $1 million means: "We're 95% confident you won't lose more than a million dollars tomorrow." It's based on models—parametric, historical, Monte Carlo—take your pick. And it's beloved by regulators and risk departments because it fits neatly into capital adequacy frameworks.

But VaR is just a guess, built on assumptions. MDD is what actually happened when things got ugly. VaR speaks to risk management and regulatory checkboxes. MDD speaks to investor psychology—how much pain a person or institution had to stomach to stay the course.

The two metrics differ in essence. VaR models the future. MDD documents the past. One helps you brace for what might come. The other shows how

[14] Also called Expected Shortfall

[15] MDD is a backward-looking, historical, *ex post* measure.

[16] *ex ante*, based on forecasts rather than actual results.

bad it got when the market last broke your heart. Used together, they provide a more complete picture—statistical foresight on one side, emotional hindsight on the other.

Meet CVaR

VaR gives a threshold—but says nothing about how bad things get beyond it. That's where Conditional VaR (CVaR), becomes useful. It answers a deeper question:

> "If we end up in that worst-case 5%, what's the average loss?"

This helps quantify tail risk—not just whether you fall off a cliff, but how far you might fall if you do.

In practice, when portfolio losses are denoted by $L = -R$, CVaR at confidence level α is defined as the expected loss conditional on exceeding the corresponding VaR:

$$\mathrm{CVaR}_{\alpha}(L) = \mathbb{E}[L \mid L \geq \mathrm{VaR}_{\alpha}(L)] .$$

This definition captures the *tail risk* beyond the VaR threshold, providing an average of the worst $\alpha \times 100\%$ outcomes. In historical simulation, the empirical CVaR is obtained by sorting observed losses in descending order and taking the mean of the largest $\alpha \cdot n$ losses, where n is the number of observations.

Example 5.1. Suppose you manage a \$100 million portfolio. Your daily 99% VaR is \$12 million: 99% of the time, losses will be less than this. But on the worst 1% of days, losses exceed \$12 million. CVaR might estimate that, on those days, the *average* loss is \$18 million. It could be more though!

□

These metrics sound precise[17]—until the assumptions behind them collapse. Both VaR and CVaR rely heavily on distributional assumptions. If the loss distribution has fatter tails than your model accounts for (as financial returns often do), both measures will underestimate the true exposure.

[17] Think of VaR like saying, "There's a 5% chance it will rain tomorrow." That tells you the cutoff—when things might go wrong. But CVaR asks, "If it does rain, how hard will it pour?" VaR gives you the boundary of bad outcomes. CVaR tells you what those bad outcomes actually look like.

In other words, if you're modeling like the world is smooth and Gaussian, and the market behaves more like a minefield, your risk estimates will be quietly wrong—until they're loudly catastrophic.

From Log Returns to Point Losses

When VaR is calculated using log returns, the result gives the loss threshold as a percentage change in log space. To turn this into a monetary value—a point loss—you need to apply an appropriate transformation to account for the exponential nature of log returns.

Suppose your portfolio value is V, and you've computed a one-day VaR of VaR_α in log-return units. The corresponding point loss is given by:

$$\text{Point Loss} = \text{V} \times \left(1 - \text{e}^{\text{VaR}_\alpha}\right)$$

This expression reflects the fact that log returns describe multiplicative changes in value. The term $\text{e}^{\text{VaR}_\alpha}$ converts the log loss back into a relative price drop, and subtracting it from 1 gives the fractional loss.

Example 5.2. Let's say you manage a \$5 million portfolio, and your 99% VaR is –0.03 (i.e., a 3% loss in log terms). Then the expected monetary loss at that confidence level is:

$$\text{Point Loss} = \$5{,}000{,}000 \times \left(1 - \text{e}^{-0.03}\right) \approx \$147{,}825$$

This means there's a 1% chance that you could lose more than \$147,825 in a single day. It's a clearer way to express risk in terms that managers and stakeholders understand—without abstract percentages, but real dollars on the line. □

Psychology Changes the Game

Risk, on paper, is tidy. Volatility, correlation, drawdown—all plotted, analyzed, optimized. Then the humans show up. They remain composed at first—silent, controlled, and waiting before any reaction appears.They just hesitate. Or press harder. A trader rides a loser longer than he should. A PM ignores the exit signal because the idea still "feels right." A team collectively decides that maybe this time the model is being too cautious.

The real danger rarely starts in the spreadsheet. It starts when people stop listening to it.

History moves in patterns—panicking with familiar rhythms, even as the details change. During the Asian financial crisis, money rushed out of emerging markets—driven not by model signals, but by urgency and the instinct to exit before everyone else. The selloff in March 2020 followed a familiar pattern: even safe assets were rapidly offloaded. The math held steady—but the people managing it reached their limits.

Inside firms, the psychology plays out in smaller scenes. The model says reduce risk. The portfolio's lagging. Someone suggests waiting a day. The warning gets buried under performance pressure, office politics, or just plain optimism.

It's tempting to think bad outcomes come from bad math. Sometimes they do. But more often, the math is fine—it just gets sidelined at the wrong moment by people who are tired, stubborn, or scared.

In the end, models don't fail alone. They usually have help—from the portfolio manager who overrides a stop-loss, the risk officer who dismisses a red flag, or the trader who trusts their gut over the signal. The math might wobble, but it's usually the human decisions around it that push it over the edge.

The Practical Quant's Guide to Risk Management

First, never assume that past volatility is a reliable indicator of future risk. The quietest periods often precede the biggest shocks.

Second, recognize that liquidity risk is as dangerous as market risk. A position that cannot be exited is a position that can destroy a portfolio.

Third, stress-test models for extreme events. Do not just ask, "What happens in a normal market?" Ask, "What happens if volatility triples overnight?"

Fourth, challenge the assumptions behind risk models. Gaussian distributions and correlation matrices fail in crises.

Finally, remember that risk is ultimately about survival. A good model maximizes returns. A great model ensures that the firm is still in business when the storm passes.

Resilience, Not Perfection

Risk management starts with accepting uncertainty. Markets move fast, models fall short, and surprises happen. The point is to build resilience—to continue moving forward when damage occurs.

Strategies get tested in calm waters, but their real shape shows up in turbulence. During disorder, the polished edges get worn off. What holds together gets used. What cracks under pressure gets shelved.

Building for resilience means choosing frameworks that keep you in the game. Imperfect systems that nonetheless reveal their limits early and remain legible under stress. Good design makes room for noise, error, and late signals.

Firms survive because they learn what breaks and adjust before it matters. They build tools that show when things are bending, long before they snap.

In the end, staying operational matters more than being precisely right. The wins come from models that can take a punch—not from ones that assume the punch won't land.

Chapter Appendix: Quantifying Risk

Computation of Returns

To apply the empirical definitions of VaR and CVaR, it's necessary to first compute the returns from the time series of portfolio values V(t). This return reflects the change in portfolio value from one period to the next.

Two common definitions of returns are used in practice:

Simple Return. The simple (or arithmetic) return is defined as:

$$R(t) = \frac{V(t) - V(t-1)}{V(t-1)} = \frac{V(t)}{V(t-1)} - 1$$

This measure directly represents the percentage change in portfolio value over one time period and is most commonly used in historical risk metrics such as VaR and CVaR.

Log Return. Alternatively, the log (or continuously compounded) return is given by:

$$r(t) = \log\left(\frac{V(t)}{V(t-1)}\right)$$

Log returns are time-additive and often used in theoretical finance and continuous-time models. However, they are less frequently used for empirical VaR calculations.

For risk estimation purposes—especially when computing historical VaR and CVaR—simple returns are preferred because they more accurately reflect realized percentage gains or losses. After computing the return series $\{R(t)\}$, we can use quantiles and tail-averaging to derive VaR and CVaR.

It is important to ensure that the time series V(t) is sorted chronologically before return computation, and that returns are calculated consistently with the intended time horizon (e.g., daily, weekly, or monthly).

One-Year MDD: A Practical Recipe

Algorithm 1 shows a procedure for computing the MDD and defines its associated parameters.

Algorithm 1 Computation of 1-Year Maximum Drawdown (MDD)

Require: Time series of past portfolio values V(t)
Ensure: Maximum drawdown value (MDD), peak date t_p, trough date t_τ, drawdown duration t_d

Extract subseries $\{V(t)\}_{t=T-252}^{T}$ for the most recent 252 trading days
Initialize $V_p(T-252) \leftarrow V(T-252)$
for $t = T-251$ to T **do**
    $V_p(t) \leftarrow \max(V_p(t-1), V(t))$
end for
for $t = T-251$ to T **do**
    Drawdown(t) $\leftarrow \frac{V_p(t)-V(t)}{V_p(t)}$
end for
Compute MDD $\leftarrow \max_t$ Drawdown(t)
Let $t_t \leftarrow \arg\max_t$ Drawdown(t)
Let $t_p \leftarrow \arg\max_{s \le t_\tau} V(s)$
Optionally, find t_r such that $V(t_r) \ge V(t_p)$
Compute duration $t_d \leftarrow t_r - t_p$ if t_r exists
return MDD, t_p, t_τ, t_d

6 Backtesting

The Art of Fooling Yourself with Style

Backtesting is where most quant strategies begin—and where many of them should end. It's the controlled environment where ideas take shape, simulations are run, and edges are imagined. At its best, backtesting helps identify patterns that might repeat. At its worst, it turns data into a mirror that reflects only what you want to see.

A clean backtest feels like progress. It gives structure to intuition and polish to strategy. The danger is mistaking it for proof.

Why Backtests Lie

A backtest is built from assumptions. Some are explicit—like which instruments to trade, or what features to include. Others are buried in code or data choices. These hidden assumptions are the ones that usually cause damage.

Market Impact In a backtest, your orders are invisible. You can buy 50,000 shares at the mid and no one blinks. The model assumes the market is a static pool of liquidity, always ready to absorb your trades without flinching.

Reality disagrees.

In live trading, size has a footprint. Push too much volume through a thin book and you don't just move the market—you become the market. The very act of executing a large order can shift prices against you, turning theoretical edge into real-world slippage. That's market impact, and it's the friction that lives between model and execution.

Table 6.1: Backtest Assumptions vs. Live Trading Realities

Component	Backtest Assumption	Live Trading Reality
Market Impact	Orders are executed without affecting price	Large orders can move the market, eroding profitability
Execution Price	Filled at mid or last known price	Slippage, latency, and partial fills distort outcomes
Liquidity	Always sufficient to match orders	Liquidity dries up during volatility; limit orders may not fill
Data Quality	Clean, survivorship-bias-free historical data	Real-time data may be delayed, noisy, or incomplete
Cost Structure	Zero or static transaction costs	Commissions, fees, and changing spreads erode returns
Stationarity	Statistical properties stay stable over time	Regime shifts break past correlations and patterns

Ignoring market impact in a backtest is misleading. A strategy that looks profitable on paper may only appear that way because it never paid the true price of its own presence.

Execution Price In backtests, trades are often filled at idealized prices—midpoints, closes, or the last observed tick. It's a convenient fiction: clean, precise, and wonderfully cooperative. The strategy says "buy," and the backtest replies, "Done. At the perfect price."

But in the real world, execution is messy.

Markets move. Quotes flicker. The price you saw when you sent the order isn't always the price you get. Between signal and fill lies a minefield of latency, queue priority, partial fills, and other participants trying to do exactly what you're doing, just a few milliseconds faster. You get slipped, front-run,[18] or simply ignored.

[18] Front-running is when someone sees or predicts your trade and places their own order just ahead of yours to profit from the price move you're about to cause.

Liquidity Backtests assume there's always someone on the other side of your trade. Want to sell 10,000 shares? Done. Want to buy at the close? No problem. Liquidity, in the model, is infinite and unconditional.

But in real markets, liquidity is a mood.

It's abundant when you don't need it and vanishes the moment you do. During stress events—earnings surprises, macro shocks, flash crashes—the bid evaporates, spreads widen, and even modest trades become market-moving. You're no longer executing; you're negotiating with panic.

A strategy that scales effortlessly in simulation may buckle under real liquidity constraints. The signal remained clear—but when it mattered most, liquidity vanished, and no one stepped in to take the other side of the trade.

Data Quality In a backtest, the data is pristine—complete, timestamped, and free of survivorship bias or lookahead bias. But real-time data is rarely that polite. It arrives late, contains errors, drops ticks, and sometimes just goes missing. Symbols change, splits get misrecorded, and historical revisions are common. If your strategy depends on the assumption that the data stream is clean and consistent, it may be building on sand. What works on a sanitized dataset can stumble badly when exposed to the chaos of a live feed.

Cost Structure Backtests often treat transaction costs as a rounding error—fixed, predictable, or worse, ignored entirely. But in live markets, costs are dynamic. Spreads widen, commissions vary by venue, and fees accumulate with volume. Add in borrowing costs for shorting, margin interest, and potential slippage, and the edge you modeled away starts to erode fast. A strategy that clears 10 basis points in simulation might net zero—or worse—once the real cost of doing business is priced in.

Stationarity Backtests often rely on the assumption that the statistical properties of the market—mean returns, volatilities, correlations—stay more or less constant over time. That's stationarity. But real markets evolve. A strategy trained on data from a bull market may crumble in a crisis. A factor that worked for a decade can vanish overnight when the macro regime shifts or the crowd piles in. Models that assume yesterday's dynamics are tomorrow's baseline risk becoming beautifully calibrated to a world that no longer exists.

The Optimization Trap

Optimizing parameters on historical data is a rite of passage for most quants—and a source of endless danger. Done naively, it produces models that shine in-sample and collapse the moment they face the future. The more knobs you can turn, the easier it is to find something that works on past data.

This is how overfitting slips in. You test dozens of configurations. You tweak lookbacks, thresholds, filters. Eventually, a combination pops out with an eye-catching Sharpe ratio. It looks like insight, but it's just an artifact of repeated sampling. The model captures idiosyncrasies of the market without any real understanding of its dynamics.

Consider a signal defined as:

$$s(t) = \sum_{i=1}^{n} w_i f_i(t)$$

where $f_i(t)$ are time-varying features (like moving averages, momentum scores, volatility indicators), and w_i are the weights. A naïve optimizer adjusts w_i until the backtest Sharpe hits 3.0. But unless there's out-of-sample validation, that Sharpe is just a reflection of how well the weights fit the noise.

It worked perfectyly—
until we hit go live.

Even simple strategies—like a moving average crossover—can be made to look like alpha with enough backtest tuning. Choose the fast and slow windows post-hoc, based on the best-performing year, and you've optimized a mirage. It won't survive contact with new data.

A well-designed backtest does indeed chase performance, yet takes care to penalize complexity, validate on unseen data, and test whether the signal survives modest perturbations. If your strategy only works when perfectly dialed, it probably doesn't work at all.

The Look-Ahead Bias Trap

Look-ahead bias ruins many strategies without leaving obvious traces. It happens when a model includes information that wouldn't have been available at the time of decision-making. This could be as blatant as using a future return, or as subtle as referencing a rating upgrade that was only published hours later.

The danger increases when timestamps aren't handled carefully. For instance, aligning data from different sources without adjusting for reporting lags creates silent leakage. A machine learning model trained this way might detect patterns that feel predictive—but only because it's cheating.

Example 6.1. A simplified example:

$$x(t) = f(y(t + 1)) + \epsilon(t)$$

Here, the model uses future returns $y(t + 1)$ to inform current features $x(t)$. The backtest performs well. The live model fails immediately.

Preventing this requires discipline. Every feature must be constructed from information available strictly before the time of trade. It also requires tools that simulate the real-world data pipeline—not just the final dataset. □

Survivorship Bias: The Hidden Trap

Survivorship bias enters unnoticed when the dataset includes only assets that are still around. Stocks that went bankrupt, funds that shut down, and instruments that were delisted quietly disappear from most databases. Backtests run on surviving constituents show returns that never existed.

Suppose you backtest a strategy on the current S&P 500 constituents, starting in 2000. The result omits every company that was removed for poor performance. That exclusion inflates performance metrics and makes the strategy look robust.

Correcting for this requires historical universe reconstruction. It means using constituent lists that reflect the exact composition at every historical point. It also means including data from failed entities—often harder to find, but essential to measure true performance.

Bias doesn't announce itself. It gets baked into the benchmark.

Transaction Costs: The Silent Killer

Backtests without costs are fantasy simulations. Markets don't offer free execution. Every trade carries friction. This includes bid-ask spreads, slippage, latency, and the market impact of your own orders.

A strategy that trades frequently might show steady gains in a costless world. In reality, each execution shaves off a piece of return. Multiply that by thousands of trades, and the edge disappears.

To model this, use impact-based cost functions. A common one:

$$C(x) = \lambda x + \eta x^2$$

Here, x is the trade size. The linear term λx captures spread and fixed costs. The quadratic term ηx^2 models slippage and market impact. This structure reflects the reality that large trades cost disproportionately more.

Even conservative cost assumptions often reduce Sharpe ratios by half. If the model breaks under realistic frictions, it was never viable.

Regime Changes: The Market's Favorite Trick (Explained)

Markets are like moody teenagers. Just when you think you've figured them out—what they like, what they hate, what gets them out of bed in the morning—they change. Again.

This, in finance-speak, is called a *regime change*. It's when the market's behavior does a 180, often without warning or explanation. One moment, it's a trending paradise where "buy the dip" feels like gospel. The next, it's a chop-fest where mean-reversion strategies reign, and trend-followers are left staring at a screen full of stop-losses.

The dangerous part? Most backtests don't see these shifts coming. Why? Because they're usually tested on one long, glorious stretch of history where

Your model's fine. What we really need is a story that backtests well.

everything looks stable. But that "stability" is often just one regime. It's like learning to drive on an empty country road—then being tossed into downtown Manhattan traffic at rush hour and wondering why your car insurance premium just tripled.

Regime Mechanics 101 Markets don't send calendar invites announcing regime changes. Sometimes the shift is structural (central banks go hawkish), sometimes behavioral (everyone suddenly loves AI stocks), and sometimes it's just weird tech stuff (hello, high-frequency trading bots). Regardless, your strategy that thrived last quarter might now be the financial equivalent of a floppy disk.

So what's a poor quant to do?

Simple: Segment your strategy across regimes. One handy way is to slice time periods based on volatility. Think of volatility as the market's mood ring—low volatility means calm and collected; high volatility means your portfolio might start stress-eating.

Now here's where it gets spicy.

Imagine your strategy's return at time t, $\rho(t)$, isn't just one blunt instrument. Instead, it's a cocktail of mini-strategies—each with its own temperament and preference for certain moods.

$$\rho(t) = \sum_{i=1}^{N} w_i f_i(\sigma(t))$$

Where:

- $f_i(\sigma_t)$: how strategy component i behaves in different volatility regimes
- w_i: the weight assigned to each component
- $\sigma(t)$: market volatility at time t

Let's simplify with two components:

- $f_1(\sigma(t)) = 1 - \sigma(t)$: Trend-following; prefers low volatility
- $f_2(\sigma(t)) = \sigma(t)$: Mean-reversion; thrives in high volatility

Assume $w_1 = 0.6$, $w_2 = 0.4$ and tabulate the calculations:

Regime	$\sigma(t)$	$f_1(\sigma(t))$	$f_2(\sigma(t))$	$\rho(t)$
Calm	0.2	0.8	0.2	$0.6 \times 0.8 + 0.4 \times 0.2 = 0.56$
Normal	0.5	0.5	0.5	$0.6 \times 0.5 + 0.4 \times 0.5 = 0.50$
Volatile	0.8	0.2	0.8	$0.6 \times 0.2 + 0.4 \times 0.8 = 0.44$

Table 6.2: Strategy returns across volatility regimes.

What Table 6.2 says is that in tranquil times, trend-following leads. In chaos, mean-reversion takes over. The model adapts—but only if the adaptation logic is robust.

A single-regime backtest is like testing your umbrella only on sunny days. It might look great on paper, but it won't keep you dry in a downpour. Markets change—often rudely and without notice. A truly robust strategy is one that flexes with market changes, adapting to shifting regimes rather than collapsing under them.

Bitcoin's Mood Swings From 2019 to 2025

If Bitcoin had a therapist, their sessions would be... eventful.

From 2019 to 2025, the world's most famous digital asset has gone through more emotional states than a caffeinated teenager—oscillating between serene optimism and full-blown panic, with a couple of existential crises in between. What's critical—especially if you're designing strategies around this

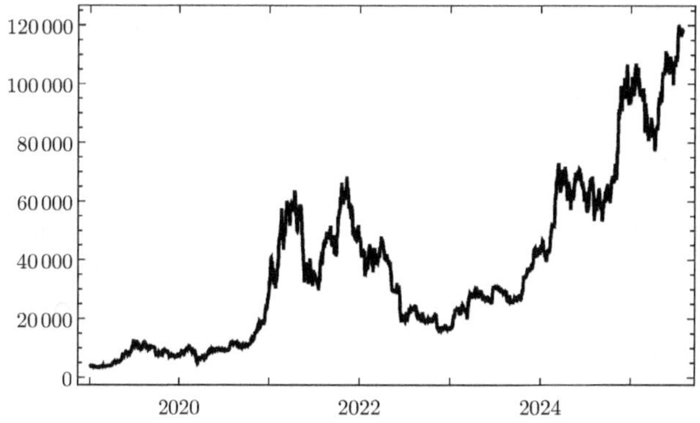

Figure 6.1: Bitcoin Price in US$: 2019-2025

asset—is to understand that each of these states, or regimes, tells a different story about market behavior, risk, and opportunity.

Period	Regime Type	Characteristics
2019–2020	Accumulation, Low Volatility	Price remained relatively flat with mild upward bias and low volatility.
Late 2020–Early 2021	Bull Market, High Momentum	Explosive uptrend begins; strong gains, high volume, and sustained volatility spike.
Mid 2021–Early 2022	Distribution, High Volatility	Price forms double-top structure, sharp pullbacks and rallies; sign of market indecision.
2022	Bear Market, Trend Reversal	Downtrend dominates; lower highs and lower lows; risk-off behavior intensifies.
2023	Consolidation, Mean-Reverting	Price stabilizes; bounces within a range; volatility compresses.
Late 2023–2025	Bull Market, Breakout Phase	Sustained upward trend resumes with sharper gains; increased market confidence.

Table 6.3: Bitcoin price regimes from 2019 to 2025.

Let's rewind Figure 6.2 plots six distinct regime changes in Bitcoin since its launch. In 2019 and most of 2020, the original crypto was the quiet kid in class—steadily gaining ground, but not really making a scene. Volatility was modest, price action was manageable, and if you blinked, you might've missed that it was even moving at all.

Then, seemingly overnight in late 2020, it morphed into the life of the party. Fueled by pandemic stimulus checks, Twitter hype, and institutional FOMO, Bitcoin surged in a parabolic rally that screamed: "we're all gonna make it." This was classic bull market behavior—high momentum, rising volume, and the general sense that Bitcoin was headed to infinity (and beyond). You didn't need a quant model—just a pulse and a Coinbase account.

But the good times don't last forever.

By mid-2021, the price began wobbling. Big spikes were followed by sharp drops. What looked like a euphoric rally started smelling a lot like a market looking for the exit. This wasn't just a blip. It was the market's way of whispering: "something's changed." And then, by 2022, that whisper became a full-throated scream. Prices tumbled, risk appetite vanished, and everyone remembered what it feels like when markets go down. This was the bear's turn to growl.

Fast forward to 2023 and things got... weirdly quiet. Prices stopped falling, but they weren't rising convincingly either. Bitcoin entered a consolidation phase—a sideways shuffle of range-bound prices, mean-reverting signals, and traders quietly muttering, "do something." If you're a strategy designer, this is the trickiest regime: it punishes both bulls and bears and leaves backtests gasping for relevance.

But just when you thought Bitcoin had settled into early retirement, it erupted again in late 2023 and into 2024–2025. A new bull cycle was underway. Prices soared, volatility returned—though this time with a hint of learned restraint. This wasn't just another rally. It was a *regime change*—a structural shift that rewrote the playbook once more.

So What? Here's the uncomfortable truth: a strategy built during one of these phases will almost certainly stumble in another.

A mean-reversion system trained on 2023 data will get steamrolled in a bull market. A momentum strategy that thrived in 2020 might blow up in 2022. And a backtest that spans only the "up-and-to-the-right" periods? That's not a backtest. It's a fantasy.

The key takeaway: strategies must flex with the market's regime. Bitcoin doesn't care how good your Sharpe ratio looked last quarter. What worked during the last bull run might be a liability in the next liquidity crunch. Mar-

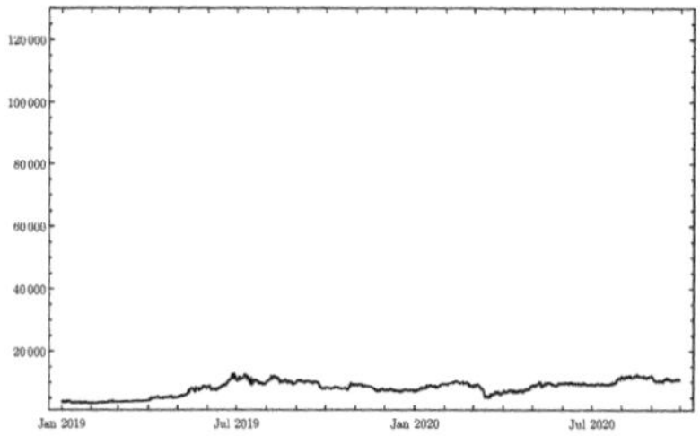

(a) Accumulation, Low Volatility

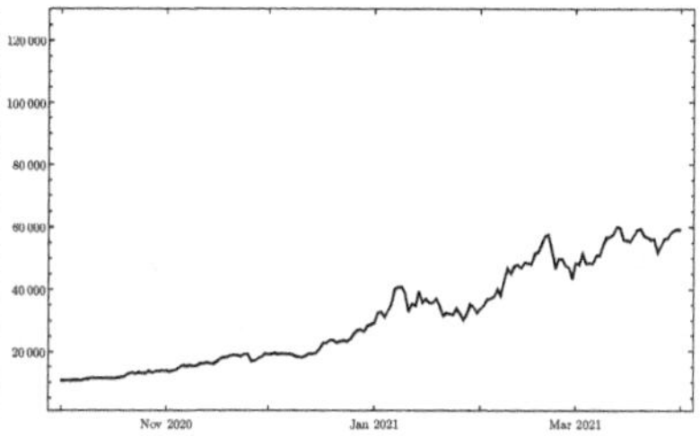

(b) Bull Market, High Momentum

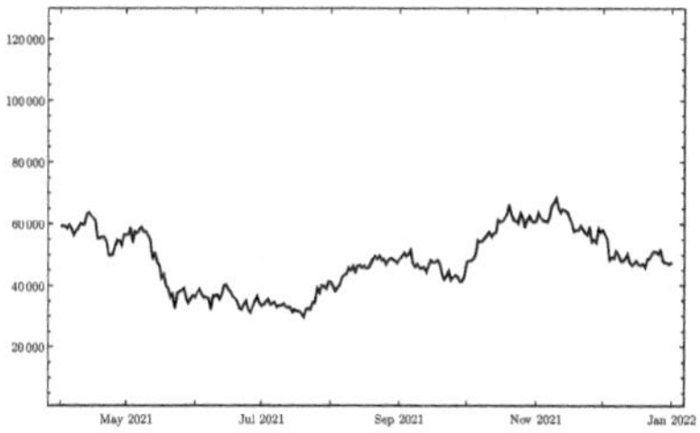

(c) Distribution, High Volatility

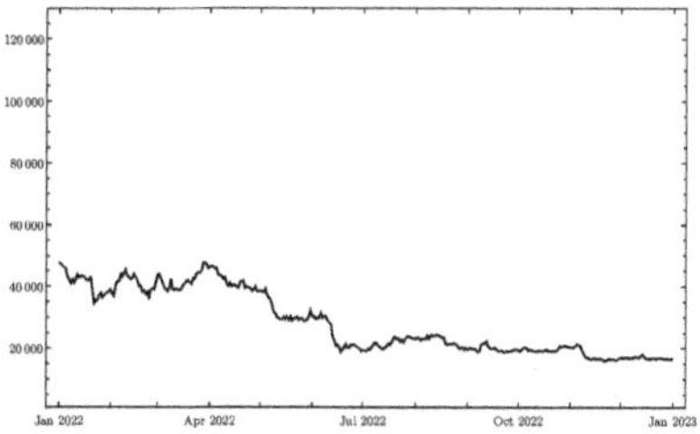

(d) Bear Market, Trend Reversal

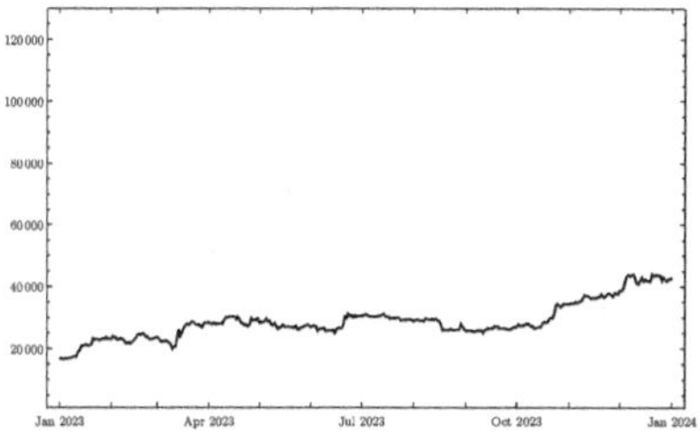

(e) Consolidation, Mean-Reverting

(f) Bull Market, Breakout Phase

Figure 6.2: The six regime changes in Bitcoin since 2019. Note that the price axes are adjusted to match.

kets change their mind, often and without warning—and your strategy better be able to keep up.

Because in the end, a robust model isn't just about predictive power—it's about survival. And survival, in the world of crypto, is the first alpha.

Precision Is Not Accuracy: Why Robustness Matters

In numerical analysis, we call a model *sensitive* when small changes in input lead to large swings in output. That's a feature of the model or the data. In finance, the models are usually sensitive. The data too. The combination is a minefield.

Take the pandemic of 2020. The S&P500 rose 15.29% that year—from 3257.85 to 3756.07. It's tempting to report that number as gospel. But does that second decimal place really mean anything?

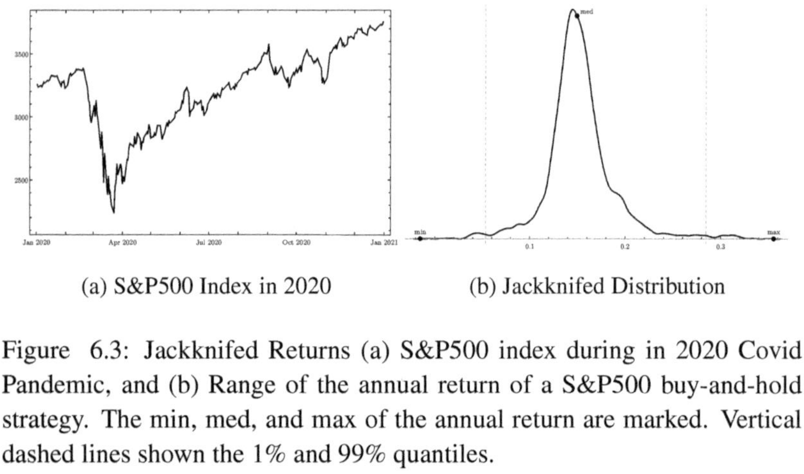

(a) S&P500 Index in 2020 (b) Jackknifed Distribution

Figure 6.3: Jackknifed Returns (a) S&P500 index during in 2020 Covid Pandemic, and (b) Range of the annual return of a S&P500 buy-and-hold strategy. The min, med, and max of the annual return are marked. Vertical dashed lines shown the 1% and 99% quantiles.

Let's test it. And "Jackknife Sampling" is one way to test it. (Berger and Skinner, 2005; Gilli et al., 2019) It's a simple idea: remove one or two data points, recompute the statistic, and see what changes. If your conclusions shift wildly, you have a problem. In finance, they often do. Especially when those points are the biggest up or down days of the year. A buy-and-hold investor who happened to miss just one of the best-performing days would have earned much less. Conversely, someone lucky enough to sidestep a crash day could look like a genius. Neither is repeatable. Both are common.

We take the daily index levels for 2020 and compute the corresponding returns. Then, we randomly delete just two days—less than 1% of the data—and recalculate the annual return. Repeat this 5,000 times. What we get is not a single return, but a distribution of outcomes. The median stays close to 15%, but the 10th percentile drops to 12%, and the 90th percentile hits 19%. The lowest result is around 2%; the highest, 45%. All from omitting just two days.

You might object that 2020 was not a typical year. Fair. But crises are not rare in financial markets—they're recurring features. And the deeper point holds: even simple return calculations are surprisingly fragile. So imagine what that means for more complex constructs—Sharpe ratios, volatility forecasts, multi-factor regressions. If the raw returns jump around this much, the conclusions we draw from them will too.

This is why point estimates in finance should always come with error bars. Reporting a return of 15.29% without a sense of the underlying variability is like calling a roulette spin a repeatable experiment. The number might be correct, but is it also robust? And robustness is what investors (and your boss) actually need.

Which brings us back to backtesting. If your strategy's appeal hinges on a precise return figure—say, 15.29% annually, net of costs—then you're probably fooling yourself. A better approach is to present a range. How much does the return change across time periods? What if a few trades go missing? What if volatility spikes?

Precision looks impressive on paper. But investors should care more about whether the result survives rough handling. If your model can't take a few punches—if it breaks when you delete a Wednesday—it isn't robust. And it isn't ready for real money.

The Practical Quant's Guide to Backtesting

Backtesting is where quant strategies go to look brilliant—until they hit the real world and promptly fall on their face. It's not that backtesting is broken; it's just that most people do it with the same reckless optimism they use to budget for vacations. They remember to pack sunscreen, but forget that it might rain. A lot.

You need to divide your data into training, validation, and testing sets. Not maybe. Not sometimes. Always. And that final test set? Lock it in a vault. Don't peek. Don't even think about peeking. It exists solely to answer the most sacred question of quant finance: "Does this actually work, or did I just get lucky with the noise?"

Then there's the matter of transaction costs. Ignore them, and your backtest becomes a fairy tale. Worse, it's a fairy tale with dragons you didn't account for—slippage, fees, spreads that widen when you're most vulnerable. If anything, overestimate your trading friction. Treat it like bad weather: it's better to bring an umbrella you don't need than to get soaked in a drawdown.

Look out for data leakage—that sneaky little bug that turns models into clairvoyants (on paper, anyway). Every feature you use must be validated for its timestamp. Ask yourself: "Would I have really known this at the time?" If the answer isn't a confident yes, throw it out. Assume your data is dirty. Because it probably is.

But here's the real kicker: markets change. They mutate. What worked in a sleepy low-volatility regime might implode when things get jumpy. Your backtest should stretch across different market regimes—fast and slow, calm and chaotic, liquid and bone-dry. If your model can't handle turbulence, it's not robust—it's just untested.

And finally, resist the urge to tinker. Every new parameter you add is another chance to overfit the past and underperform the future. Complexity looks clever. But simplicity survives. The fewer knobs you have to turn, the fewer ways you have to fool yourself.

Done right, backtesting is both science and skepticism. It's where you test not just the strategy—but your own ability to be honest about what you're seeing.

What a Good Backtest Really Is

A backtest offers a hypothesis—framed in historical data and shaped to explore how an idea might perform under known conditions. It equips you for the future—by helping you explore scenarios, test assumptions, and ask the questions that matter most.

The best backtests are the most honest. They resist complexity unless it's earned. They penalize flexibility. They include slippage, impact, and the possibility that the market doesn't care about your signal. They don't just model what worked—they test what might still work when the world moves on.

And even then, they fail sometimes. That's the price of realism.

7 Socratic Finance

Dialogs on Bugs, Precision, and Accuracy

If there were one person I wish I'd had as a mentor when I first began my career in computational science, it would be Forman Sinnickson Acton. Acton, a mathematician and engineer with a deep skepticism of black-box thinking and a gift for clarity, authored two of the most important books on numerical computing I've ever read: *Numerical Methods That Work* and *Real Computing Made Real*. (Acton, 2005, 2020) His voice—dry, incisive, and impatient with nonsense—feels as relevant now as ever.

Acton went above and beyond just teaching how to compute. He taught how to think critically about computation—how to anticipate numerical pitfalls, question algorithmic assumptions, and respect the limits of floating-point arithmetic. His lessons went beyond code and into the habits of mind essential for reliable, meaningful scientific work.

The following fictional Socratic dialogue imagines what it might have been like to speak directly with Acton. The questions are mine; the answers are modeled on his writings. What follows is part homage, part conversation I wish I'd had—and still try to live by.

Me Professor Acton, help me out—why should I lose sleep over numerical errors? My code runs clean, no crashes, no complaints.

Acton Ah, but that's like saying your parachute is fine because it worked on the ground. Programs that "run fine" may simply not have been asked the right questions—or the hard ones. Have they been subjected to harsh, difficult, or adversarial conditions—the kind of challenging scenarios that reveal weaknesses and flaws. Have you tried feeding them the wolves?

"Beware the invisibility of numerical errors."

Me I mean, sure—maybe things go sideways in some freak edge case. But how often does that really happen?

Acton Rare? That's what the Titanic thought about icebergs. Let me introduce you to errors of the *third kind.* Not typos. Not bugs. These are insidious—logical sinkholes buried deep in your algorithms. You won't see them until your program either crashes like a diva or quietly lies to you with straight A's.

Me Alright, hit me with a real-world example.

Acton Gladly. Picture this: you're solving $x^2 - 10^5 x + 1 = 0$. Plug that into the standard quadratic formula and watch what happens. You end up subtracting $10^5 \pm \sqrt{(10^5)^2 - 4}$. Those two terms are nearly identical—subtract them, and you've just flushed your significant digits down the precision drain. Instead, you should use a reformulated version—compute one root with the standard formula and get the other by $\frac{c}{a \cdot x_1}$. It's like switching to snow tires before the storm hits.

Me So this is all just an implementation problem?

Acton Not just implementation, but more comprehension. You can write clean code and still get garbage results if you don't grasp how your algorithm behaves numerically. Try starting an iterative method with a lousy guess and see how far it doesn't go. Sometimes it crawls, sometimes it bolts—straight into a wall. Take Newton-Raphson, for example: start too far from the root or near a point where the derivative vanishes, and it can oscillate, diverge, or converge to something meaningless. Worse, it might converge—to the wrong answer—so quietly you won't notice until the damage is done. The point is getting an answer and knowing whether that answer deserves to be trusted.

Me Should I just rely on software to handle these cases?

Acton Not without caution. Software follows the instructions you provide—its output shaped entirely by how you define the problem. If your formulation is flawed or your algorithm unstable, no amount of library calls will rescue you. It will compute whatever you ask, even if what you ask makes no numerical sense. Worse, modern software often hides the warning signs—ill-conditioning, loss of significance, convergence issues—under layers of abstraction. You get an answer, but no insight into its validity. Blind reliance on software is automation without understanding.

Me How can I improve my numerical intuition?

Acton Start by sketching your functions. Geometry is as important as algebra, especially when your algorithm depends on how rapidly something changes—or how often it doesn't. A quick plot can reveal discontinuities, flat spots, steep slopes, or asymptotes that will make life hard for any numerical method. Take $f(x) = \tan(x)$ near $\frac{\pi}{2}$—if you're using Newton-Raphson and you land too close, the derivative blows up and the method diverges instantly. That's not bad luck, it's bad foresight. Next, run controlled experiments. Perturb your inputs slightly and watch how the output responds. If a small nudge sends your results into orbit, you've found sensitivity—often the first warning sign of trouble. Read your residuals, test extreme cases, and don't stop at "it runs"—ask yourself if it behaves. Intuition comes from pattern recognition earned through repetition and scrutiny.

Me And what about preserving precision in computations?

Acton You preserve precision by respecting where it tends to vanish. Reformulate any expression that risks subtracting nearly equal numbers or dividing by something precariously small. For example, when evaluating $\sqrt{x^2+1} - 1$ for small x, direct computation loses significant digits. But rewrite it as $\frac{x^2}{\sqrt{x^2+1}+1}$, and the digits stay where they belong. Series expansions, rational approximations, even basic algebraic manipulation—these aren't academic exercises, they're how you keep your results from quietly degrading into noise. Precision isn't just about more digits; it's about not squandering the ones you already have.

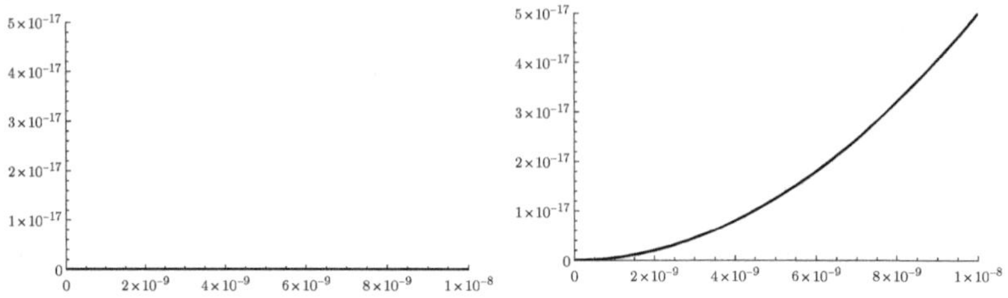

(a) $\sqrt{x^2+1}-1$ (b) $\frac{x^2}{\sqrt{x^2+1}+1}$

Figure 7.1: Comparison of two equivalent expressions over a small domain around $x = 0$. While mathematically equivalent, (a) suffers from catastrophic cancellation for small x, resulting in significant numerical error. The reformulated version shown in (b) maintains stability and preserves precision across the domain.

Me I don't get it.

Acton Of course you don't—most people don't until they lose a few digits and wonder where they went. Look closely at $\sqrt{x^2+1}-1$ when x is very small, say 10^{-8}. Mathematically, it evaluates to something near 5×10^{-17}, but numerically? You're subtracting two quantities so close together that the result gets swamped by floating-point error. That's catastrophic cancellation. You see blank if you plot it as in Figure 7.1a . Now, rewrite it as $\frac{x^2}{\sqrt{x^2+1}+1}$. It's the same expression, algebraically, but this version doesn't subtract nearly equal values, so it preserves significant digits giving results like in Figure 7.1b. Computers just follow orders. If your instructions destroy precision, the computers won't stop you.

Me Does this difference matter to quants?

Acton Yes, and not just a little. In finance, you're often working with derivatives, sensitivities, and optimizations where small changes in input can mean large changes in output. When evaluating near-zero quantities—say, the time value of an option near expiration—subtracting nearly equal numbers can wipe out precision and give you nonsense. Imagine mispricing a derivative by a few basis points because your code couldn't handle small differences cleanly. Traders won't call it a floating-point error; they'll call it a loss. Precision errors in pricing models, Greeks, or risk metrics don't just matter—they compound.

Me But isn't all this kind of tedious? Why not just crank up the precision and be done with it?

Acton You can throw more digits at the problem—but if the algorithm is wrong, all you get is a more precise mistake. Quadruple precision won't save you from bad logic or unstable formulations. Precision isn't a brute-force fix; it's a resource. Use it wisely, or you'll just be computing nonsense to 34 decimal places instead of 16.

Me What about choosing algorithms? Are there general guidelines?

Acton Choose algorithms that match the problem's geometry and characteristics. Test them thoroughly under extreme conditions, and never trust an algorithm blindly.

Me What about choosing algorithms? Any rules of thumb that actually hold up?

Acton Start by choosing algorithms that reflect the structure of your problem—don't force a square solver into a round equation. Stability, convergence behavior, sensitivity to inputs: these aren't afterthoughts, they're the selection criteria. Then stress-test it. Try extreme inputs, bad guesses, degenerate cases. If it breaks, better now than when it's running live. And no, never trust an algorithm just because it came from a textbook or a software package. Test first, believe later.

Me So it's really just about building better habits?

Acton Precisely. Most errors aren't accidents—they're consequences of shortcuts taken too early. Understand the problem before you touch a keyboard. Simplify the formulation, isolate the sensitive parts, and plan for what might go wrong. The best debugging is done before you write the bug. Prevention always costs less than repair—in time, accuracy, and credibility.

Me Thank you, Professor. I see now that precision in computing isn't just technical—it's philosophical.

Acton Correct. It's about discipline, judgment, and knowing when your numbers lie. Now get back to your code—and this time, make it think.

Precisely Wrong

Before diving and delving into another round of models, metrics, and market mechanics, let's pause for a reality check.

"Never make anything more accurate than it needs to be. Better be approximately right than precisely wrong."

Finance, for all its equations and optimizers, still has a knack for being absurd in the details. Like how a portfolio can shift its annual returns by a full percentage point just by changing the day it rebalances. (Gilli et al., 2019) Now that's calendar roulette!

To get at the heart of this fragility—the kind that hides behind decimal points and confidence intervals—consider the following exchange. It's fictional, yes, but every line has been field-tested by reality. Sometimes the quickest way to the truth isn't through another proof. It's through a conversation.

Enrico Tell me, would you say precision is the holy grail of financial modeling?

Me I suppose so. Precision means our math is airtight. That's got to be good, right?

Enrico Sure, assuming the math is marching in the right direction. But let's say I give you GPS coordinates calculated to the eighth decimal point. . . and they guide you expertly to the wrong Starbucks. Would you still be grateful for the precision?

Me No, I'd be annoyed. Precision doesn't help if you're precisely lost.

Enrico Exactly. So, can we agree that precision isn't always virtuous? That perhaps—just perhaps—we should care about being right, not just exact?

Me Yeah. That makes sense. Accuracy—being correct—seems more important than just being precise.

Enrico Good. Now, let's shift to the financial realm. These beautiful, math-laden models we build—do you think they're always grounded in reality?

Me Not really. They often make simplifications—about how investors behave, or how markets move.

Enrico Right. So if the foundation is flawed—say, we assume everyone's rational when they're actually panic-scrolling Twitter—how much comfort should we take from a mathematically pristine outcome?

Me Not much. A precise answer to a wrong question is still wrong.

Enrico Bingo. Precision, in that case, becomes a kind of intellectual vanity. Let's dig deeper: When we talk about model errors, what do you think we usually mean? Calculation bugs? Rounding quirks?

Me That's my guess. Tiny numerical slip-ups?

Enrico Those exist, yes. But more insidious are empirical errors—the kind that arise when our models misrepresent reality. For example, how do most models define "risk"?

Me Typically as variance—how much returns bounce around.

Enrico And does that match how investors actually think about risk?

Me Not exactly. Investors are happy with volatility if it means big gains. It's the downside that hurts.

Enrico Precisely. (Pun intended.) Variance punishes both losses and windfalls equally, which makes sense mathematically and zero sense behaviorally. That's an empirical error—a mismatch between model and world. So what's our recourse?

Me Maybe... tweak the assumptions?

Enrico That helps. But we also lean on heuristics—know what those are?

Me Rules of thumb? Simple strategies that work well enough?

Enrico Exactly. Heuristics don't chase perfect. They chase useful. Why might that be smart?

Me Because perfect can be a trap. A heuristic might find a good solution faster—and avoid dead ends like local minima.

Enrico You're catching on. Heuristics often involve randomness—trial and error writ large. That sounds risky, no?

Me Yeah, I'd worry about inconsistent results.

Enrico So we run the heuristic many times, treat its outputs like a distribution, and look for stability. If it gives us robust results, we don't need perfection. Just reliability. Fair trade?

Me Definitely. That feels more honest than chasing a false sense of certainty.

Enrico Speaking of false certainty—here's a little-known but jaw-dropping fact: shifting the day a portfolio rebalances—literally just moving it from, say, Monday to Friday—can alter its annual returns by up to a full percentage point.

Me Wait, seriously? You're telling me that the day of the week—a purely arbitrary choice—can shift performance that dramatically? That seems... absurd.

Enrico Absurd, yes. But also true. And that absurdity is precisely the point. You'd expect financial returns to hinge on market dynamics, economic signals, maybe even central bank policy. But Tuesdays? That feels more like astrology than asset management.

Me So the implication is that the precision we worship in modeling—down to basis points and optimized risk-weightings—is built on sand if it's that sensitive to something as trivial as the calendar?

Enrico Bingo. This is what's known in technical circles as a "fragile optimization." You optimize your portfolio to perfection—minimize risk, maximize Sharpe ratio, maybe even align with your star sign—and then, boom, one minor tweak and the whole edifice wobbles. Imagine building a cathedral with a laser-guided chisel. . . on a Jell-O foundation.

Me That's kind of terrifying. It means we might be overfitting not just to data, but to quirks. To noise disguised as signal.

Enrico Exactly. The illusion of control. It's a comforting lie, especially for quants and portfolio managers who like their spreadsheets tidy and their models deterministic. But reality doesn't always cooperate. Markets are stochastic beasts. They don't care about your calendar settings.

Me So then—what's the alternative? Just accept the randomness? Throw our hands up and rebalance whenever the coffee machine breaks?

Enrico Not quite. The point isn't to abandon rigor. It's to be humble about it. Build models that aren't so sensitive to trivial inputs. Use robust methods. Stress test. Embrace slightly less precision if it means much greater resilience. Think of it like engineering a bridge: you don't want the structure to collapse just because someone gained five pounds or it rained Tuesday instead of Thursday.

Me So precision that breaks under pressure isn't precision—it's a liability. It's precision cosplay.

Enrico That's one way to put it. True robustness is messy. It's about designing for the unexpected, not just the expected. So yes, a one-percent swing from a rebalancing tweak is absurd. But it's also a flashing red light: beware the illusion of precision. Especially when your inputs are chosen by habit, not principle.

Enrico Exactly. Financial models are sensitive beasts. So tell me: if a model is that fragile, does it matter how precise the numbers are?

Me Not at all. Precision without durability is pointless.

Enrico Then let's wrap it up with an old saw that still holds water: In finance, as in life, it's better to be approximately right than precisely wrong. Sound fair?

Me More than fair. That might just be the best heuristic of all.

The Tyranny of Tuesdays

There's something quietly deranged about the fact that shifting the day a portfolio rebalances—from, say, Monday to Tuesday—can alter its annual returns by up to a full percentage point. One percent. Gone or gained, depending on which weekday your Excel macro prefers.

Let that marinate for a second. We spend entire careers trying to eke out basis points from factor tilts and volatility filters, yet here's a calendar quirk that can rival the impact of a central bank press conference.

It sounds like finance crossed with astrology. ("My portfolio underperformed because Mercury was in retrograde and I rebalanced on a Thursday.") But it's not a joke. It's an empirical result observed in live portfolios and backtests alike. What you're seeing is not just noise. It's an artifact of how markets behave in time, and how models—especially those high on precision and low on humility—interact with that behavior.

Precision vs. Fragility This is where the steel beam of quantitative precision meets the hairline crack of real-world fragility. Quants love to optimize: maximize the Sharpe ratio, minimize drawdowns, tweak your parameters until the model sings in tune. But here's the problem: many of those optimizations are brittle. Change the tempo—rebalance weekly instead of monthly, or shift the rebalancing window by a few days—and suddenly your elegant, mathematically blessed portfolio is having a nervous breakdown.

A one-day shift shouldn't matter. A real strategy can withstand the shift from Wednesday to Thursday without its performance falling apart; anything less is just a statistical party trick. Worse, it's a dangerous one, because it seduces you with its apparent rigor. "Look how clean my backtest is!" you say, unaware that your model is a sandcastle built during low tide.

The Calendar Isn't Neutral At some point, someone must have noticed it by accident. A junior quant, maybe, staring at a spreadsheet late at night, tweaking the rebalancing schedule because they were curious—or bored—and watching the portfolio's return jump like a startled cat. Monday produced one number. Tuesday, another. Shift the model forward by a single day, and you weren't just nudging returns—you were rewriting them.

This wasn't supposed to happen. The calendar was meant to be a backdrop. But there it was: the day you chose to update your portfolio—an arbitrary, clerical detail—could nudge your supposedly scientific model by an entire percentage point. Which in the performance-obsessed world of finance is the difference between genius and mediocrity, bonus and pink slip.

People tried to explain it. Some blamed "market microstructure," a phrase that sounds like science but mostly just means "we don't know, but it probably has to do with how trades settle." Mondays were sleepy, Fridays frantic, midweek some hazy mean. Others pointed to the calendar clustering of economic reports, or the psychological hangover that markets carry into different days. And all of that may be true, to a point.

But here's what's actually alarming: it doesn't matter which day does it. It matters that any day can. That the model—a gleaming artifact of logic and data and spreadsheet sorcery—can be thrown off by something so banal. A genuine strategy holds firm no matter what day it is; one that changes with the calendar is simply an overfit hunch pretending to be serious.

Robustness Over Elegance This is where the heuristic mindset earns its keep. A model should be robust rather than perfect. It needs to work under slightly different conditions, tolerate weird inputs, and keep humming when reality throws curveballs. The best models are the most adaptable. They work like sturdy hiking boots built for all terrain.

And this is the quiet, uncomfortable truth about financial modeling: precision is often just a way to decorate our ignorance. A kind of high-resolution guesswork. A model that responds to something as arbitrary as the day of the week is fragile.

So What Do We Do? We build models that acknowledge their own limits. We test them under alternative assumptions. We jiggle the inputs—rebalancing days, lookback windows, factor definitions—and see what breaks. And if something does break? Good. That's your model telling you where it's pretending to know more than it does.

The markets are not deterministic systems. They're not clocks. They're weather. A model that changes with the day of the week is tantamount to guessing.

The paradox of financial modeling is that the more you seek precision, the more brittle your models become. Tuesday doesn't follow your formula. The market doesn't either. The solution is to apply care in a new direction, to be careful in a different way. Prioritize generalizability over elegance. Prioritize resilience over beauty. Test your assumptions like a grumpy auditor. Celebrate models that are "boring but robust."

8 AI in Finance

A Trader's-Eye View from Inside the Machine

Everyone in finance talks about AI now. It's on pitch decks, in job descriptions, and somewhere in your inbox there's a startup promising to "redefine alpha " using it. But what are we really talking about?

Start broad: AI is the umbrella term. It means machines doing things that usually require people—like spotting patterns, making decisions, or pretending they understand language. But in quant work, when someone says "AI," they usually mean one of its more grounded and useful children: Machine Learning (ML) or Deep Learning (DL).

Machine Learning ML algorithms can infer computational rules from data. You give it data, it finds relationships. Not magic, just statistics with a gym membership. A quant might use ML to forecast volatility, detect outliers in a limit order book, or optimize factor weights. It's especially good at problems where the rules shift subtly over time but not so fast that all memory is useless.

ML can, in a sense, be thought of as a kind of pattern hunter. You feed it data, and it sets about, with no prior knowledge of your intent, searching for the rules that link one observation to another. In this way, it can seem as though it has an innate knack for discovering the rules by which your data lives. But the trick is this: it doesn't truly "know" these rules in the way humans might. It simply nudges and tunes its internal machinery until it can mimic the patterns it has seen before. The quality of its discoveries depends entirely on the quality of the data you give it; feed it noise, it will learn noise, and feed it bias, it will learn bias. And what it learns are never timeless truths, but patterns that may hold tomorrow, or may vanish with the next dataset. So yes, ML finds relationships in data, but it does so blindly, bound to what it's shown, and forever at the mercy of the patterns we ourselves have captured.

Deep Learning DL is ML's flashier, more attention-grabbing younger sibling, the one who turns up to family gatherings with stories of self-driving cars and talking machines. Where the older sibling often needs a hand — carefully crafted features, painstakingly chosen by human experts — the younger one insists on doing it alone. Give it the raw data, and it will burrow through layer upon layer of neural connections, finding patterns in numbers, building its own understanding from the ground up. This self-reliance is part of its allure, but also its weakness; without a mountain of examples and the computational muscle to sift through them, its brilliance falters. Still, when the conditions are right, DL's talent for unearthing meaning from the raw and the unrefined can make even its older sibling pause in admiration. Feed DL enough price charts and it starts building its own idea of what a head-and-shoulders pattern looks like—even if it doesn't call it that. DL shows up in sentiment analysis (reading the market's mood through headlines), voice-to-text parsing of earnings calls, and anything else where structured models can't quite keep up.

What Quants Actually Use Most quants aren't chasing HAL 9000. They're using algorithms to rank trading signals or forecast short-term flow. Sometimes it works. Sometimes it doesn't. But the real edge comes from understanding which tool fits which job. ML shines when you have features and need predictions. DL shines when you have noise and need features. AI, in the end, is just a fancier way of asking: What if the model learned instead of you?

Of course, the boundary between ML and DL isn't always strict. Many real-world systems combine them. You might use a deep learning model to extract sentiment from unstructured text, and then feed that signal into a machine learning model that decides whether it belongs in a trade. These hybrid approaches—ensembles that let each method play to its strengths—are increasingly common in production trading systems.[19]

And if you're wondering what the machines actually understand—ask them to explain their trades. That'll tell you everything you need to know.

[19] In practice, many modern quant workflows blend ML and DL. For example, an ensemble might use ML for structured price features and a DL network for sentiment extracted from news headlines—each model learning what it learns best.

Table 8.1: ML vs. DL in Practice

Category	Machine Learning	Deep Learning
Data Type	Structured (tables, features, factors)	Unstructured (text, images, raw prices)
Training Size	Works well with small to medium datasets	Requires large datasets to generalize well
Use Cases	Factor ranking, risk modeling, trade signal classification	Sentiment analysis, audio transcription, pattern recognition
Speed to Train	Fast, often seconds to minutes	Slower, often hours or more
Overfitting Risk	Moderate — depends on model complexity	High — especially with small data and deep networks

DL made the call, ML took the blame, and AI still won't explain.

Why Everyone's Suddenly a Data Scientist

AI, once the stuff of hedge fund slide decks and tech conference buzzwords, has formally crash-landed in quantitative finance. The promise? Uncanny foresight, seamless execution, and godlike portfolio intuition—all coded neatly in Python. We're told that deep learning models now whisper market forecasts with startling precision, that reinforcement agents can outwit human traders in timing execution, and that sentiment analysis can parse the mood of Twitter before the market sneezes.

But walk onto a trading floor—or what's left of one in this Slack-and-screenshare era—and you'll hear a different tune. Beneath the buzz lies a deeper unease. For traders, many of these AI marvels feel less like magic and more like a high-stakes trust fall into a black box. The tools are powerful. But are they empowering?

Let's take a closer look.

Table 8.2: AI Use Cases in Trading

Use Case	What It Says It Does	What the Trader Sees
Price Prediction	Forecasts asset prices via LSTMs, transformers, and ensemble tricks	Slick models, sure—but often overfit, slow to adapt, and rarely explainable
Portfolio Optimization	Chooses allocations based on return-risk calculus	Ignores macro gut-checks, political shocks, and the "human tape"
Execution Algorithms	Times orders using reinforcement learning	Opaque, brittle, and biased in ways you often discover after a blow-up
Sentiment Analysis	Uses NLP to mine market-moving emotion from text	Noisy, delayed, and a step behind anyone watching Bloomberg with sound on
Risk Management	Anticipates tail risks, estimates VaR	Useful until someone asks why—and the model shrugs in tensors and weights

The Trader's Top 5 AI Grievances

From a trader's perspective, here's where the models break: not in their math, but in their metaphors—tools built to navigate stationary worlds get lost in shifting regimes; algorithms that claim objectivity still carry the biases of the data they were fed; and perhaps most crucially, models that predict without explaining leave traders holding the bag when markets go sideways and risk managers come knocking. The failure is technical, strategic, temporal, and psychological. AI may be excellent at finding patterns, but it still doesn't know which ones "matter." And when the model falters, it's the human—battle-tested, blinkered, and occasionally brilliant—who has to clean up the mess.

Black Box Blues To a machine learning engineer, model opacity is a technical challenge. To a trader, it's a career hazard. When the market turns and the model fails (and it will), someone has to answer for the drawdown. "It seemed confident" doesn't play well with risk committees.

The Regime Problem Markets aren't stationary. They lurch from low-volatility calm to macro panic with little warning. AI, trained on yesterday's calm, tends to misfire under today's chaos. Human traders, with their annoying habit of watching CNBC and remembering 2008, still have the edge in adapting on the fly.

Strategic Deskilling Here lies the existential crisis: AI rewrites the very definition of a trader. Where once a senior PM shaped strategy, now they babysit a model. For veterans, this feels less like augmentation and more like exile from the cockpit.

Timing Is Everything (And Models Are Late) High-frequency trading is measured in milliseconds. Even in less frantic contexts, timing matters. Many AI-driven strategies introduce latency via overengineering—turning what should be nimble into something sluggish and fragile. Like trying to day-trade with a Roomba.

Overconfidence and Drift Machine learning models have limited shelf-life. What works in one regime often unravels in another. Without constant retraining and rigorous oversight, models drift—quietly and dangerously. Human traders, flawed as they are, tend to recalibrate instinctively. Models won't scream when they're wrong. They won't blink or hesitate. They'll just quietly give you the wrong answer while you're busy trusting the math. Always stay one step ahead of them.

"Chill. My training data had this covered."

What's the Way Forward?

The paradox is that AI in finance is at once indispensable and untrustworthy. Its computational power is undeniable, its insights occasionally sublime. But left unchecked, it risks becoming a technocratic mirage—offering certainty where none exists.

The most promising setups we've seen? Hybrid systems, where AI serves as an advisory engine rather than an autonomous pilot. Traders retain the wheel, models whisper suggestions, and together they navigate markets with both precision and prudence.

Better yet, emerging fields like XAI and causal ML offer hope that these models might one day tell us why they think what they think—a necessary evolution if we're ever going to use them in real-world, capital-at-risk decisions.

Firms that treat traders and quants as collaborators—not as legacy code and progress, respectively—will have the strategic advantage. Everyone else will be fighting the last market regime with yesterday's model.

Co-Pilot, Not Autopilot

AI is changing the DNA of trading. But whether this is a revolution or merely an evolution depends on your vantage point.

From the trader's side of the screen, the tech often feels like a dazzling intern—fast, tireless, occasionally brilliant, but frequently clueless about the big picture. And entirely unprepared to answer when things go wrong.

The future is AI working alongside traders—each focused on what they do best to make smarter, faster decisions together. One finds patterns. The other knows when to ignore them.

Why Traders May Be the Real Bottleneck in Quant Finance

Let's start with the romantic myth: the seasoned trader, sleeves rolled up, reading the tape, sensing a shift in the market's mood before the models catch wind of it. It's compelling. It's cinematic. It's also, increasingly, obsolete.

In an environment defined by information speed, computational scale, and statistical nuance, human intuition is not just fallible—it's inefficient. AI, despite its imperfections, offers new capabilities. The real challenge may lie with humans relying on instincts shaped by a different era—trying to match machines with tools and hunches honed for a different era.

Intuition Doesn't Scale Traders argue that their edge lies in pattern recognition and experience. But what is a neural net if not an engine of pattern recognition—trained not on a few decades of desk-side memory, but on millions of data points, market regimes, and price moves? A human might notice a pattern over the course of a few months. A model notices it in nanoseconds—and tests its validity across decades. A trader's edge stays with the trader and seldom scales. AI, properly engineered, can scale—across markets, across time zones, without sleep.

Humans Are Slow, Biased, and Overconfident The psychological literature here is brutal and unrelenting. Traders—like all humans—are vulnerable to confirmation bias, recency bias, anchoring, and emotional overreaction. AI models? They may be flawed, but at least they're consistently flawed, and their biases can be audited, not just denied. Even when AI fails, we can trace the lineage of its failure: the features it over-weighted, the assumptions it carried forward. When a trader blows up a position, the postmortem is usually just: "I thought it would bounce."

AI Doesn't Panic In 2020, when Covid hit the markets like a meteor, human traders did what humans do: they panicked. They dumped, they froze, they second-guessed. Models, on the other hand, kept calculating. They didn't need bathroom breaks. They didn't watch CNBC in horror. They just kept processing data—and in many cases, recovered their composure faster than their human counterparts. When markets went haywire in March 2020, many hedge funds that had bet on volatility got clobbered—their models simply couldn't keep up with the chaos. But not everyone got burned. A few, like Gammon Capital, a New York AI-powered hedge fund managed by my friends Larry Richards and Mike Mescher, went up 600%. (Fletcher and Henderson, 2020)

Experience Is Not a Hedge Against Change Many senior traders pride themselves on having seen "every kind of market." But history, as every data scientist knows, is not always a great predictor of the future—particularly when the future involves novel instruments, algorithmic dynamics, and non-linear market structures that didn't exist 10 years ago. Experience may teach resilience, but it can also breed rigidity. Meanwhile, AI models retrain. They adapt. They forget the wrong things on purpose.

The Best Traders Are Already Cyborgs The most effective market participants today aren't Luddites on one end or quants on the other—they're hybrids. PMs who trust their models, who interrogate outputs but don't override them without reason, and who understand that alpha is now co-authored by humans and machines. Traders who resist this shift—who insist that "gut" will always win—are fighting the last war. The smart ones are evolving.

Maybe It's Not the Model That Needs Explaining

Much is made of AI's "black box" problem. But maybe the more pressing issue is the human black box: traders who can't quite explain why they made that call, or what data justified their conviction.

In a world increasingly driven by accountability, auditability, and measurable edge, that kind of opacity is a luxury no longer tolerated. So if traders are feeling disempowered, maybe it's not because the models are too opaque—but because, for the first time, their own opacity is being challenged. So if traders are feeling disempowered, it may be because their intuition-driven decisions are now being challenged, for the first time, by models that bring new levels of visibility.

> Would you trust your money to a model that can't explain itself?
> Fair question.
> But here's a better one: Would you trust it to a human who also can't—but insists they "just know"?

9 The Mirage of the Mean

The Dangerous Charm of Averages

If I were tell you the average depth of a river is three feet, would you cross it?[20]

If you answered yes, congratulations: you're either a golden retriever or someone who has never met statistics in the wild. Because what I didn't tell you is that this particular river is one foot deep at the banks and twelve feet deep in the middle. And unless you're amphibious—or on stilts—you're going for a swim.

This is what statistician Sam Savage and Harry Markowitz (Savage and Markowitz, 2009) has coined the flaw of averages: the idea that a single, tidy number can encapsulate a messy, chaotic world without leading you into the deep end. It's the statistical equivalent of "Sure, that parachute probably works."

Averages are seductive. They whisper simplicity, order, clarity. GDP per capita! Average test scores! Mean time between catastrophic system failures! They give us a number—a truth, allegedly. But averages are also like those friends who tell "mostly true" stories that leave out crucial details.[21]

Let's step back and look at the mathier underbelly of this problem. Because not all means are created equal. Some are born to summarize; others to mislead. There are at least three kinds of average you need to know about—

[20] Sam Savage and co-authors posed a similar question in the wonderful book *The Flaw of Averages*.

[21] You won money in Vegas? Fantastic. You didn't mention you also mortgaged your cat.

arithmetic, geometric, and harmonic—and each one is waiting for you to use it in the wrong place so it can silently ruin your conclusions.

"Technically, the average loss is well within tolerance."

The Arithmetic Mean—Simple, Seductive, and Occasionally Stupid

The arithmetic mean is the one you know and love—or at least use reflexively in Excel.

You add up your values, divide by how many there are, and voilà: a number. Test scores? Add them. Rainfall? Add. Your blood pressure over the last ten family dinners? Yep, still add.

Example: $(80 + 90 + 100) \div 3 = 90$.

Easy. So easy, in fact, that we forget what it assumes—namely, that each value is pulling equal weight. Which, in real life, is rarely the case.

Let's say Jeff Bezos walks into a dive bar where 20 people are sipping well whiskey and arguing about fantasy football. Suddenly, the average income in the bar jumps to something north of a billion dollars. But has the bar really gotten wealthier?

No. What happened is the arithmetic mean got mugged by an outlier. And now it's lying on the floor next to your naive assumptions.

The arithmetic mean spreads everything evenly—like a socialist peanut butter that doesn't care if you're a saltine or a loaf of sourdough. Which works just fine when things are evenly distributed. But when the data has sharp elbows? You're gonna want something sturdier.

The Geometric Mean—When Numbers Multiply Behind Your Back

Meet the geometric mean: the arithmetic mean's nerdier, more introverted cousin—the one who shows up to family reunions with a slide rule and a chart of exponential decay, and who (despite the social awkwardness) often turns out to be the one telling the truth about your finances.

The geometric mean matters when things compound: money, bacteria, awkward silences in meetings. Take this simple scenario: you invest \$100. Year one, it grows by 50%. Year two, it drops by 50%. The arithmetic mean pipes up cheerfully:

> Hey, (–50% + 50%)/2 = 0%. You broke even!

But no. You now have \$75. You lost money. And this is where the arithmetic mean's helpful façade begins to unravel like discount hosiery.

Here's what really happened:

Year 1 $\$100 \times 1.5 = \$150$
Year 2 $\$150 \times 0.5 = \$75$

To decode this decline, we summon the geometric mean:

$$\sqrt{1.5 \times 0.5} = \sqrt{0.75} \approx 0.866$$

This implies a compound multiplier of 0.866—or, more soberingly, an annualized loss of about 0.134, which is equivalent to 13.4%.

Why does this matter? Because compounding cares about sequence and magnitude. A 50% gain followed by a 50% loss doesn't leave you where you started. The loss lands on a larger amount, dragging the total down further than the gain pulled it up.

Each year, your money effectively shrank by a factor of 0.866, which equates to a –13.4% annual return:

$$0.866 - 1 = -0.134$$

So, while the arithmetic mean smiles and says "zero percent change," the geometric mean quietly does the math and shows you lost 13.4% each year, compounded.

The arithmetic mean gives you an average that ignores compounding. The geometric mean gives you the rate that actually happened. For investments—and anywhere else numbers pile on top of each other—the geometric mean tells the truth, even if it's not what you wanted to hear.

The Harmonic Mean—The Hero of Rates, the Enemy of Intuition

Now for the underdog. The one with pocket protectors and zero chill: the harmonic mean.

This "mean" is the go-to when you're dealing with rates. Think: speed, cost per unit, efficiency. It doesn't get the love it deserves because it's not intuitive—and frankly, it's a little needy. But when rates vary over a fixed quantity (say, distance), the harmonic mean is the only one that won't lie to your face.

Suppose you drive 60 miles at 30 mph, then 60 miles back at 60 mph. What's your average speed?

If you said 45 mph, congratulations: you're wrong. Here's why:

Leg 1 $60 \div 30 = 2$ hours
Leg 2 $60 \div 60 = 1$ hour
Total 120 miles in 3 hours = 40 mph

The harmonic mean gives you:

$$\frac{2}{\frac{1}{30} + \frac{1}{60}} = \frac{2}{\frac{3}{60}} = 40$$

It gives more weight to smaller values—which makes sense: slower speeds dominate your travel time. Just like your cheapest investments dominate your cost per share, and your most awkward interactions dominate your memory of a party.

When Averages Attack

Let's bring this home with a financial horror story. You're a fund manager. (Congrats, you're now a PowerPoint abuser with a Bloomberg terminal.)

Your fund goes up 20% in Year 1, then down 10% in Year 2. Arithmetic mean says: "That's a 5% average return."

Except your investor starts with $100 and ends with:

Year 1 $\$100 \times 1.2 = \$120$
Year 2 $\$120 \times 0.9 = \$108$

That's a net gain of 8%. So what annual return would actually explain that? Geometric mean comes to rescue:

$$\sqrt{1.2 \times 0.9} = \sqrt{1.08} \approx 1.039 \Rightarrow 3.9\% \text{ per year}$$

The arithmetic mean told a pretty story. The geometric told the truth.

Geometric vs. Arithmetic: A Cautionary Tale from the Fund of Funds

It looked like a straightforward exercise. A fund of funds (FoF) had spread its capital evenly across five hedge funds in a single year. The results were in: –8%, –2%, 10%, 13%, and 25%. One of the interns—keen, spreadsheet fluent, maybe a little too quick on the draw—suggested taking the geometric mean. "It gives the true compounded return," she said. "Isn't that what matters?"

It's not a bad instinct. The geometric mean is, in fact, the right tool—when you're tracking returns over time, where each period's outcome becomes the starting point for the next. But that wasn't what happened here.

This was not a case of compounding. The capital was allocated across five managers simultaneously, with no sequencing from one to the next. The FoF placed equal-sized bets on all five hedge funds, and let them run for a year. No reinvestment. No rebalancing. No path.

So we ran the numbers the right way.

First, we adjusted each hedge fund's return for their 2 and 20 fees—2% management plus 20% incentive, with the incentive fee calculated on gains net of management:

- The –8% fund lost money. After a 2% management fee, the investor was down –10%.
- The –2% fund also lost money. Post-fees, it dropped to –4%.
- The 10% fund, after fees, returned: $(0.10 - 0.02) \times 0.8 = 6.4\%$
- The 13% fund gave: $(0.13 - 0.02) \times 0.8 = 8.8\%$

- The 25% fund produced: $(0.25 - 0.02) \times 0.8 = 18.4\%$

Now take the arithmetic mean:

$$\frac{-10\% + (-4\%) + 6.4\% + 8.8\% + 18.4\%}{5} = \frac{19.6\%}{5} = 3.92\%$$

Then came the FoF's own fees: 1% management and 10% incentive on what remained.

- After the 1% management fee: $3.92\% - 1\% = 2.92\%$
- 10% incentive on that is 0.292%
- Net return to investors: $2.92\% - 0.292\% = 2.628\%$

The intern was puzzled. "But the geometric mean gives a lower number," she said. And that's exactly the point.

The geometric mean assumes sequencing. It acts as if you put your money in Fund A, then moved it to Fund B, and so on, compounding year after year. That's not what happened here. This was a portfolio snapshot, not an exposure to sequential returns. The capital was placed once, split evenly, and held simultaneously.

Using the geometric mean in this setting creates more than a rounding issue. It applies the wrong concept to the structure of the investment. You'd be treating a diversified portfolio like a time machine. This would be a mistake.

The lesson is simple: use the geometric mean when time is the axis. Use the arithmetic mean when capital allocation is. Don't let the elegance of a formula seduce you into forgetting how the money actually moved.

Cheat Codes for the Perplexed

So when should you use which?

Arithmetic mean: You're adding stuff up that's evenly weighted—test scores, grocery bills, average number of times your cat ignores you.

Geometric mean: When you're dealing with growth, decay, or anything that compounds over time—like investments or fungal infections.

Harmonic mean: When you're averaging rates—price per unit, miles per gallon, or how many spreadsheets your intern can crank through per hour.

But more importantly: ask what story you're telling. Averages are mathematical tools that shape narratives—framing how we interpret patterns, compare outcomes, and make decisions with data. Use the wrong one, and you're writing fiction in your quarterly report.

Bob's Quantitative Faceplant

Now let's meet Bob. Fund manager. Poker enthusiast. Self-assured to a fault.

At the annual "Quant & Chips" poker night, Bob tells anyone who'll listen that he's rocking a 60% win rate on trades. Swagger is poured like bourbon. What he doesn't say is that:

- His $10K trades win 70% of the time
- His $1M trades win 30% of the time

His arithmetic average win rate means nothing. His money-weighted return? Even less flattering.

What he needed was a weighted mean—or, more precisely, to think in terms of harmonic mean logic, where trade size (like distance in speed problems) changes the entire average.

Bob's 60% win rate? A numerical hallucination. The kind that gets you laughed out of poker night and investigated by compliance.

Truth and Consequences

Bob learns his lesson the hard way—on the river, literally and figuratively. Alice, a soft-spoken quant with the deadly calm of someone who teaches stochastic calculus for fun, flips over a better hand. And then gently explains to Bob that win rates without context are just vibes.

Alice You're averaging over trades, but the trades aren't equal. You weighted your ego, not your exposure.

Bob (Blinking) So my win rate is ...

Alice Useful only if you're trying to impress a spreadsheet.

Mean Deception

To his credit, Bob doesn't rage-quit. He runs the numbers the next day. Correctly. Weighted by dollar exposure.

His fund's "performance" shrinks by half. The good news? He stops misleading his investors. The better news? He starts learning which average tells the right story.

He even begins footnoting his reports. Progress.

Now a little puzzle. You're driving 30 miles. Half the distance at 30 mph, half at 10 mph. What's your average speed? Most people will say 20 mph.

But again, distance is fixed—time isn't.

$$\text{Harmonic mean: } \frac{2}{\frac{1}{30}+\frac{1}{10}} = \frac{2}{\frac{4}{30}} = 15$$

Fifteen. Because slowness drags everything down. Just like misapplied averages.

Seduced by Simplicity

We crave clarity. And averages promise it: one number to rule them all. But clarity without context is just confidence wearing blinders.

The arithmetic mean? Helpful, but naive.
The geometric mean? Quiet, but correct for growth.
The harmonic mean? Awkward, but honest with rates.

So the next time someone offers you an average, don't just nod. Ask: Which kind? What's being averaged? And is this telling the truth—or just rounding it off? Because averages aren't answers. They're stories.

And as with rivers, poker, and hedge funds, you'd better know what's beneath the surface before you wade in.

10 Quant Survival and Beyond

How to Stay Sharp, Stay Sane, and Eventually Move On

Quant finance looks clean on paper: efficient markets, Gaussian assumptions, tidy code. But a career in it? That's messy. It's shaped by performance reviews as much as performance, by politics as much as precision. Some days, your sharpest risk model won't matter as much as the narrative someone else tells about it in a meeting.

This chapter is about what happens when the math ends and the human stuff begins. It's about the subtle art of surviving inside the machine—managing up, absorbing blame, spotting when incentives turn toxic. But it's also about what happens when you start looking beyond the machine.

Because for many quants, the story doesn't end at the desk. Skills honed in finance—probabilistic thinking, systems intuition, risk awareness—turn out to be highly portable.Whether you end up in tech, policy, academia, or your own venture, the real career arc centers on adaptability—on knowing when to shift your focus toward meaning, growth, and long-term impact.

Survival inside finance takes sharpness. Thriving beyond it takes perspective.

The Reality of Office Politics in Quant Finance

Quantitative finance is about more than models, data, and strategies. Success often hinges on navigating the murky waters of office politics, intellectual property protection, and career sustainability. New quants frequently enter the industry believing their mathematical and technical brilliance will automatically translate into recognition and advancement. The reality is far more complicated, and often more disappointing.

Models alone rarely determine career trajectories. Understanding human dynamics, knowing when to guard intellectual assets, and positioning oneself strategically can be just as vital. This chapter explains how the most successful quants adapt, survive, and ultimately thrive beyond mere technical mastery.

Every quant who enters finance imagines a meritocracy, where performance and technical prowess decide success. Unfortunately, quant roles often involve considerable politics. Performance is important, yet perceptions, relationships, and internal influence frequently determine opportunities and advancement.

Imagine two quants: the first is exceptionally gifted mathematically but struggles to communicate insights effectively to traders and executives. The second quant, though technically competent, focuses more energy on relationships and effective communication, carefully aligning their ideas with traders' workflows. Over time, the second quant typically sees more opportunities and recognition. The first quant, despite superior technical skills, might remain stuck in a research role without broader influence.

Effective quant practitioners understand that convincing colleagues of an idea's value is as crucial as developing the idea itself. They know that models don't sell themselves, and recognize the necessity of framing results clearly and persuasively. These interpersonal skills don't detract from technical expertise; rather, they amplify a quant's overall effectiveness and influence.

Alpha Theft: Protecting Your Intellectual Property

Alpha theft is an uncomfortable but persistent issue within finance. Quants routinely see their best ideas copied, repurposed, or even outright stolen. The typical scenario involves a junior quant creating a profitable signal or strategy, only to discover later that another team or individual is using a slightly modified version without acknowledgment.

This can occur subtly—perhaps a senior colleague dismisses an idea in a meeting, only to quietly implement something similar months later. Or it can be blatant—a fellow quant directly presents someone else's strategy as their own. Either way, the original author of the idea rarely sees proper credit or reward.

"In this game, blame is the only metric."

To combat alpha theft, quants should document their research and methods carefully, clearly establishing ownership and authorship of intellectual contributions. Moreover, being strategic about sharing information is critical. Sharing just enough to demonstrate value—but withholding key implementation details—can ensure colleagues rely on the original creator for execution. Additionally, creating proprietary methods or custom data processing steps, difficult for others to replicate independently, provides natural protection.

Ultimately, the strongest defense against alpha theft is making oneself indispensable. The more essential a quant's skills and insights become, the harder it becomes for others to appropriate ideas without recognizing the quant's ongoing value.

The Trader-Quant Relationship: A Delicate Balance

The relationship between traders and quants frequently contains tension, largely because the two groups approach risk and markets differently. Quants rely on rigorous analysis, probabilistic reasoning, and statistical validation. Traders, meanwhile, often rely heavily on experience, intuition, and rapid judgment.

Conflicts arise when a model-generated signal contradicts a trader's gut instinct. Traders may dismiss the model outright, frustrating the quant who sees clear mathematical support for their conclusions. This friction isn't necessarily adversarial; traders possess valuable market insights and intuitions that models don't capture fully, such as short-term liquidity conditions or immediate flow dynamics.

Successful quants build a strong understanding of traders' perspectives—using every disagreement as a chance to improve. Effective quants frame recommendations in practical terms, clearly explaining how a model complements rather than competes with a trader's experience. A good quant never demands blind obedience to a model; instead, they offer tools that enhance traders' existing judgment and execution capabilities.

The best trader-quant relationships are partnerships, built on trust and respect for the strengths each party brings to the table. Quants who recognize and actively cultivate this dynamic thrive far more readily than those who insist that technical rigor alone is sufficient.

Career Moats: Making Yourself Indispensable

Quantitative finance is fiercely competitive, making career longevity challenging. Automation constantly threatens routine tasks, and firms continually seek cost reductions through outsourcing or simplification. Quants whose roles are limited to maintaining legacy models or standard workflows risk being replaced by software, cheaper labor, or simpler approaches.

To survive, quants must build career moats—unique expertise or skills that are difficult or costly to replace. Proprietary knowledge represents one such moat: if only one quant understands a critical trading model's nuances, replacing them is extremely difficult. Developing specialized expertise in complex areas such as market microstructure or exotic derivatives pricing similarly provides powerful protection.

Additionally, combining modeling skills with operational capabilities dramatically enhances job security. A quant who both designs models and manages their real-world implementation becomes deeply embedded in firm infrastructure. Similarly, quants who build strong relationships across teams, ensuring widespread recognition of their unique value, find themselves far less vulnerable to restructuring or replacement pressures.

Career moats don't appear automatically. They require proactive effort, strategic planning, and deliberate positioning. The most successful quants constantly evaluate their roles, refining skills and establishing expertise areas that provide long-term career resilience.

The Practical Quant's Guide to Career Longevity

Being a brilliant quant gets you in the door. Staying in the building? That's another skill set entirely.

The careers that last aren't built solely on code and clever math. They're built on range. Quants who understand market structure, trader behavior, and the politics behind a PnL survive the long haul. The ones who think their model speaks for itself usually don't.

Longevity, it turns out, has a lot to do with translation. Can you explain your insight in one sentence to someone who doesn't know what stochastic means? Can you sit in a meeting and defend your signal without sounding like you're defending your ego?

And then there's credit. In an environment where information is currency, documenting your contributions is more than diligence—it's insurance. That innovative execution model you built? Someone's going to repackage it at some point. Make sure your fingerprints are on the original.

Careers plateau when people stop learning. The best quants keep adding skills—new languages, new domains, new ways of thinking. They don't wait for the firm to hand them a mandate. They evolve before the strategy expires.

And perhaps most crucially, they invest in people. Allies in trading, risk, and upper management aren't just nice to have. They're survival gear. When politics flare up—as they inevitably do—it helps to have someone at the table who knows you're more than a spreadsheet.

Longevity in quant finance follows the logic of a dynamic system—shaped by adaptation, feedback, and continuous recalibration over time. The smart ones treat their careers the same way they treat their models: monitor, adapt, and always hedge against downside.

Enduring Quant Life

Sustained success in quantitative finance demands far more than superior mathematical talent or computational skills. It requires strategic awareness, interpersonal insight, adaptability, and proactive career management. Quants who integrate these dimensions as essential complements to their technical core build lasting careers—adapting, excelling, and influencing the field over time.

Ultimately, the quant who endures is one who sees beyond mere equations, perceiving the human context in which financial modeling inevitably occurs. A lasting career is built on more than models—it draws strength from communication, context, and the ability to apply insights where they matter most. Navigating the broader landscape of relationships, influence, intellectual property, and career strategy provides the real foundation for long-term success in quant finance.

Beyond the Terminal

Quantitative finance careers are intense and rewarding—but rarely indefinite. While many enter quant roles drawn by intellectual challenge and lucrative pay, the reality of long hours, relentless pressure, and rapid technological and market shifts can shorten tenure. Even the most talented quants frequently begin to wonder what comes after finance. Unlike other professions, where career longevity can increase with seniority, quants regularly face obsolescence as their skills commoditize or automation encroaches.

Eventually, nearly every quant must confront the question of what comes next. Recognizing career paths beyond trading terminals, identifying transferrable skills, and preparing strategically for transitions are crucial for sustainable professional lives. This chapter outlines common pathways quants pursue post-finance, highlights skills that transfer readily to other sectors, and offers practical guidance for managing the transition beyond the trading desk.

Why Most Quants Do Not Stay Forever

Few quants remain in finance for their entire career. Multiple factors typically lead to shorter tenure, beginning with burnout. The quant role demands constant intellectual energy, requiring continual model improvement, adaptation to evolving markets, and responding rapidly to failures. These pressures accumulate, eventually leading many quants to seek more sustainable and less stressful alternatives.

Compensation dynamics also play a role. While finance offers high earnings initially, compensation growth tends to flatten over time for quants compared to portfolio managers, executives, or traders. Firms continuously automate or outsource quant tasks, limiting career advancement opportunities and salary growth, leading many experienced quants to reconsider their futures.

Intellectual stagnation can occur as well. Many quants enter finance from academic or scientific backgrounds, attracted initially by challenging problems and significant resources. Over time, the initial intellectual excitement can diminish, replaced by repetitive tasks such as debugging models, routine backtests, or incremental optimization. When creative exploration slows, quants often seek intellectually richer environments outside finance.

Industry instability further encourages exits. Shifts in market structure, new regulatory regimes, and evolving technologies regularly disrupt quant roles, rendering specialized knowledge quickly obsolete. Quants who built careers around particular technologies or strategies find themselves at risk when those approaches become outdated or replaced.

The Common Exit Paths for Quants

When quants leave finance, several predictable pathways emerge. Portfolio management provides a natural progression, especially for quants with broader economic insights or strong risk management skills. Moving into a portfolio management role demands a different skill set—market intuition, macroeconomic reasoning, and strategic decision-making—but it leverages quantitative analysis foundations effectively.

Another common path is fintech or broader technology roles. The quantitative skills developed in finance transfer naturally into technology-driven startups, established software companies, or data-driven enterprises. Quants frequently find fulfilling roles designing machine learning algorithms, managing large-scale data infrastructures, or driving innovation in sectors like cybersecurity, blockchain, or artificial intelligence.

A return to academia or research is also frequent, especially among PhDs. Quant experience often strengthens subsequent academic or research careers, providing real-world perspectives, substantial data analysis expertise, and clear awareness of practical constraints. Roles teaching quantitative finance or computational mathematics or conducting applied research at universities or think tanks can be particularly rewarding.

Entrepreneurship offers another compelling pathway. The analytical rigor, problem-solving capability, and technical proficiency developed in quant finance provide strong foundations for launching startups. Quants who build successful ventures frequently apply their quantitative insights to data analytics, automated trading platforms, AI-driven tools, or digital financial services. The transition into entrepreneurship leverages both analytical depth and the proactive risk-taking mindset cultivated in finance.

Finally, some quants achieve financial independence early and retire outright. Successful careers at hedge funds or high-frequency trading shops can create sufficient wealth for early retirement, allowing quants to pursue personal interests, philanthropy, or quieter lifestyles outside markets altogether.

Transferrable Skills: What a Quant Can Do Elsewhere

A few years in quantitative finance leaves you with tools you can carry almost anywhere. The most obvious is comfort with data—real, messy, uneven data. You've cleaned it, sliced it, run models on it, and argued over what it means. That ability to turn raw numbers into insight works just as well in technology, healthcare, consumer analytics, or public policy as it does on a trading desk.

Programming is another passport. Most quants pick up more than one language—Python, R, C++, maybe some Java—plus the habits that make code hold up under pressure. You've probably worked with data pipelines, visualization tools, and statistical libraries. Those skills slide neatly into data science, software engineering, machine learning, cloud computing, or a technology startup that needs someone who can turn ideas into running systems.

Risk management travels well, too. Once you've learned how to measure uncertainty and think about worst-case scenarios, you can bring that mindset to insurance, cybersecurity, corporate strategy, or supply chains. Any field where a bad surprise can be expensive is a place where that discipline pays off.

And then there's the problem-solving muscle. The habit of breaking big, tangled problems into smaller ones, testing solutions, and refining them isn't limited to finance. It fits in logistics, operations research, manufacturing, or anywhere else people wrestle with complex systems that don't behave nicely. The same thinking that helps you debug a Monte Carlo simulation can help someone schedule a fleet of trucks or keep a factory line running.

The Challenges of Leaving Finance

The skills travel easily; the exit doesn't always. Outside the industry, a lot of hiring managers still picture quants as market-bound specialists—brilliant with pricing models, but maybe not much else. That means you have to do

"I escaped the desk, but volatility still haunts me."

the translating yourself. Strip out the desk slang, reframe your experience, and show how the same thinking that priced options can guide a product launch or untangle a supply chain.

Culture is another curveball. Finance runs on speed, competition, and a scoreboard that updates in real time. Other industries often move slower. Decisions take weeks, not hours. Feedback comes in quarterly reviews instead of daily PnL. Incentives can be fuzzy, with success measured in influence or process improvement rather than dollars made today. Adapting means recalibrating your pace, your patience, and sometimes your definition of "urgent."

Money can be the hardest adjustment. Quant finance pays more—sometimes a lot more—than academia, government, or many tech roles. A job outside might be richer in freedom, creativity, or stability, but lighter on bonuses. That trade-off is easier if you've already decided what you're optimizing for.

Then there's identity. Many quants define themselves by their technical edge and direct market impact. Moving into a role where wins are counted in research citations, product launches, or strategic milestones can feel like switching sports entirely. It takes time to settle into new rules, new scoreboards, and new ways of measuring your own value.

Planning an Exit Strategy

Successful career transitions don't occur spontaneously. Strategic preparation significantly increases likelihood of success. Quants should actively build professional networks outside finance early, attending industry events, conferences, or engaging in communities related to technology, research, or entrepreneurship.

Broadening technical skillsets beyond finance-specific applications further supports successful transitions. Learning new technologies, mastering advanced machine learning techniques, or exploring emerging analytical frameworks positions quants effectively for varied future roles.

Additionally, seeking cross-functional roles within finance can enhance marketability outside it. Involvement in risk management, operational improvement, or technology development projects demonstrates versatility, enhancing quants' resumes for potential external employers.

Financial preparation also matters. Quant careers frequently provide early financial advantages, but few subsequent roles match finance's peak earnings. Building financial cushions early provides greater flexibility in accepting initially lower-compensation positions elsewhere, reducing immediate financial pressures during transitions.

Some exits from finance are quiet migrations rather than flameouts. One day you're modeling tail risk in a volatility surface, the next you're optimizing ad bids at a tech company or launching a startup built on stochastic magic. The truth is, the quant's toolkit travels well.

Quantitative skills—discipline with data, fluency in risk, a feel for systems—aren't chained to finance. They belong to a broader tribe of technical problem-solvers. Industries from healthcare to policy analysis, from AI startups to academia, are hungry for people who can stare at uncertainty and make decisions anyway.

But here's where it gets tricky: finance teaches you to price everything, including yourself. And outside of finance, the compensation curve may not spike as sharply. That's okay. Some of the best post-finance careers aren't about maximizing comp—they're about maximizing meaning. A sense of mission, intellectual stretch, or the simple joy of building something that doesn't live in a spreadsheet.

Leaving the Street doesn't mean losing your edge. Many who exit keep a toe—or a Bloomberg terminal—still connected. The markets are always there. You might come back. Or you might find that what you learned trading risk is what makes you valuable somewhere else.

Transitions are rarely tidy. They require patience, humility, and the willingness to not be the smartest person in the room—at least for a little while. But for quants who stay adaptive and curious, there's plenty of life beyond the PnL.

And it might even come with fewer compliance trainings.

What Happens Next

Quant careers don't last forever. Strategies decay, volatility dries up, firms get acquired. But the tools—the sharp math, the clean code, the instinct for risk—they endure. The smartest quants don't just master the game; they plan for what comes after.

They build moats that outlive market regimes: intellectual agility, technical fluency, and a sense of where the world's headed next. They don't just react when roles vanish or bonuses shrink—they anticipate. They pivot before the desk does.

And they know better than to define themselves by a job title or a PnL line. What they're really trading in is adaptation. Pattern recognition. The ability to wrangle complexity and extract signal—no matter the domain.

In the end, the most resilient quant is the one who evolves beyond the model—adapting as the landscape shifts, learning new tools, and expanding their perspective. Because the real career isn't bound to a terminal. It's what you do after you close it.

A Wolfram for the Functionally Curious

Guiding the Pythonically Perplexed

It's safe to assume you already speak Python. After all, Python is the go-to language for data science, modeling, and quantitative work. Then you open WL, the Wolfram Language, and something feels offish. Square brackets instead of parentheses. Loops seem to have disappeared. Everything looks like as an expression.[22]

That strangeness is the entry point. Here symbolic computation is the default. Interactivity is built in. Functional programming flows in a way that feels less forced and more organic.

This appendix (gently) walks you through that transition.[23]

No need to pull away from Python. The aim here is to give you a few habits and mental tools to think in the WL Language. You know lists, functions, mappings, lambdas, and loops. In what follows, you'll meet their symbolic and often more powerful counterparts.

The path is simple. Each step ties to what you already know while exposing the deeper logic of WL's world. What looked foreign at first will grow familiar. You'll see why many scientists, engineers, and quants keep a Math-

[22] In this appendix, I may seem to use WL and Mathematica interchangeably, so let me clarify. WL is the programming language, while Mathematica is the software environment that runs it, complete with the notebook interface, visualization tools, and everything else you need to interact with your code. You code in WL, and Mathematica is where you use the code. Consider Python and Jupyter: Python is the language, Jupyter is the interactive environment where you work with it.

[23] I've put this entire appendix in a notebook so that you can run the code snippets and see WL in live action via Mathematica.

ematica notebook open next to their Python IDE. It becomes less a substitute than a lab for symbolic thinking—where complex ideas shrink into manageable form, and simple ideas take on unexpected depth.

The Language of Everything

In WL, everything is an expression. Numbers, symbols, functions, graphics, and data all share this single form. Once you see that, the language feels like LEGO. Each expression is a block. Blocks connect, and bigger structures appear without friction.

The rule is simple. Every piece of code has the form

```
Head[arguments]
```

This applies everywhere. Functions follow it. Arithmetic follows it. Data structures and plots follow it too.

Suppose you'd like to add 2 and 3, so you enter `2 + 3`. Internally to WL, this becomes `Plus[2, 3]`. The head is `Plus`. The arguments are 2 and 3. The output is 5.

Or `Sin[Pi/2]`. Here the head is `Sin`, and the argument is $\pi/2$.

Even a set of numbers `{1, 2, 3}` is stored as `List[1, 2, 3]`, wherein `List` is the `Head` and the argument is `1,2,3`. Graphical functions also follow this model. The code `Plot[Sin[x], {x, 0, 2π}]` has a head `Plot` and two arguments: the function to plot and the domain.

Once you grasp this pattern, you can predict how new objects are built.

To see how WL really stores an expression, use `FullForm`. For instance,

```
FullForm[f[a + b]]
```

returns `f[Plus[a, b]]`. That is the structure the kernel works with.

The rule is absolute: every construct in WL is an expression with a head and some arguments. Other languages, such as Python, split these ideas into different kinds of syntax. WL collapses them into one model. Once you treat expressions as the building block, the language becomes easier to read, debug, and extend.

Embracing Functional Programming

In most languages, functional programming is added as an extra layer. Python, for example, relies on `lambda` or `map` to provide what Wolfram handles directly. In the Wolfram Language, you can define functions anonymously, apply them to lists, and even treat them as symbolic expressions to manipulate.

A pure and anonymous function is an unnamed function written with the # symbol for arguments and & to close. For example:

```
#^2 &
```

This defines a function that squares its input. You can apply it directly:

```
#^2 &[5]
```

to get the result 25.

To map across a list, use `/@`:

```
(#^2 &) /@ {1,2,3,4}
```

This yields `{1, 4, 9, 16}`. In Python terms, that is like `map(lambda x: x**2, [1,2,3,4])`.

Another operator is `Apply` (@@), which swaps the head of an expression with a function:

```
Plus @@ {1,2,3}
```

The result is 6.

You can also define reusable functions. `SetDelayed (:=)` makes them evaluate when called, while `Set (=)` evaluates them immediately. For example:

```
f[x_] := x^2
```

Now `f[3]` returns 9.

In the Wolfram Language, functions are expressions like any other, so you can assign them to variables or include them in lists. For instance:

```
g = (# + 1 &) ;
g[4]
```

Here, `g` stores a pure function that adds one to its input. Entering `g[4]` applies the function and returns `5`.

Moreover, because functions are expressions, you can store them in data structures like lists. For example:

```
f1 = (#^2 &);
f2 = (# + 3 &);
funcs = {f1, f2};
funcs[[1]][5]
```

This evaluates to `25` because `funcs`⟦1⟧ retrieves the first function in the list, which squares its input.

Storing functions in lists lets you apply them selectively, iterate through them, or build pipelines of operations, just as you would with numbers or strings. The Wolfram Language treats them all as symbolic expressions.

By now you've probably noticed that in Wolfram, brackets carry specific meanings tied to the symbolic structure of the language.

Single square brackets `[]` are used for function application. When you write `f[x]`, you are applying the function `f` to the argument `x`. This is the standard way to call any function, whether built-in or user-defined.

Double square brackets ⟦⟧ are used for part extraction.[24] They retrieve elements from lists, tables, and other expressions with internal structure. For example, `list`⟦3⟧ returns the third element of `list`. If `list = 10, 20, 30`, then `list`⟦3⟧ evaluates to `30`.

Think of `[]` as "apply" and ⟦⟧ as "index." They serve different roles: one runs a function, the other digs into a structure. Misusing them is a common source of error for new users.

Symbolic Computation is the Default

Differentiation, integration, algebraic manipulation, and equation solving are native features of Wolfram. In Python, you reach for libraries like `SymPy`. In Mathematica, every expression is already symbolic.

Most languages assume numbers. They expect concrete values, and symbolic work is extra. Wolfram flips this. By default, `x` and `y` are treated as

[24] In pure text mode, ⟦ ⟧ shows as [[ ]].

algebraic symbols. The system manipulates them exactly as written, holding off on evaluation unless you ask.

This gives you direct access to calculus and algebra. For example:

```
D[x^3 + x^2, x]
```

returns `3 x^2 + 2 x`. Partial derivatives work the same way:

```
D[x y + x^2, x]
```

gives `y + 2 x`.

Integration is symbolic too:

```
Integrate[Sin[x]^2, x]
```

returns

```
x/2 - 1/4 Sin[2 x]
```

which in LaTeXwould look like $\frac{x}{2} - \frac{1}{4}\sin(2x)$.

You can reshape expressions with tools like `Expand`, `Factor`, and `Simplify`. Try

```
Expand[(x + 1)^2]
```

to see that it produces:

```
(1 + x)^2
```

Equations can be solved symbolically as well:

```
Solve[x^2 + x - 6 == 0, x]
```

gives

```
{{x → -3}, {x → 2}}
```

For solving simultaneous equations, enter:

```
Solve[x + y == 7 && x - y == 1, {x, y}]
```

and get the pair:

```
{{x → 4, y → 3}}
```

Be careful with using the symbol `N`. It's reserved by WL for when you want numbers. You can use `N` to get a numerical approximation for $\sqrt{2}$:

```
N[Sqrt[2]]
```

which produces `1.41421`. If you don't use `N`, then Mathematica keeps exact forms, like $\sqrt{2}$. That preserves precision and avoids rounding errors until the last step.

Symbolic computation is the default in the Wolfram Language. You can differentiate, integrate, solve, and simplify expressions without imports or conversions. For Python users used to numeric-first behavior, this unlocks a different style of work—algebra first, numbers later.

`Manipulate` for Instant Interactivity

`Manipulate` is one of the most useful features of WL. It lets you wrap an expression in a dynamic interface with sliders, menus, or input fields, instantly turning static code into something interactive. With it, you can build visualizations, simulations, or simple dashboards in real time.

In most programming environments, interactivity means importing libraries, wiring up widgets, and managing callbacks. In WL, it is native. A single line of code with `Manipulate` creates a live plot you can drag and adjust.

This makes it easy to explore how mathematical expressions respond to parameter changes. It is well suited for sensitivity analysis, prototyping, and visual explanation. Unlike Python, interactivity in WL is a direct extension of the language itself.

Consider a simple parabola:

```
Manipulate[Plot[a x^2, {x, -10, 10}], {a, 1, 5}]
```

This creates a plot of the function ax^2 like in Figure A.1 and gives you a slider to control the value of a. As you move the slider, the graph updates in real time.

`Manipulate` does more than plotting graphs. It can work with any expression: numbers, text, graphics, or simulations. For example:

```
Manipulate[FactorInteger[n], {{n, 1, "Integer"}, 1, 100, 1}]
```

computes the prime factorization of numbers from 1 to 100. Figure A.2 shows two instances for factoring integers 15 and 68.

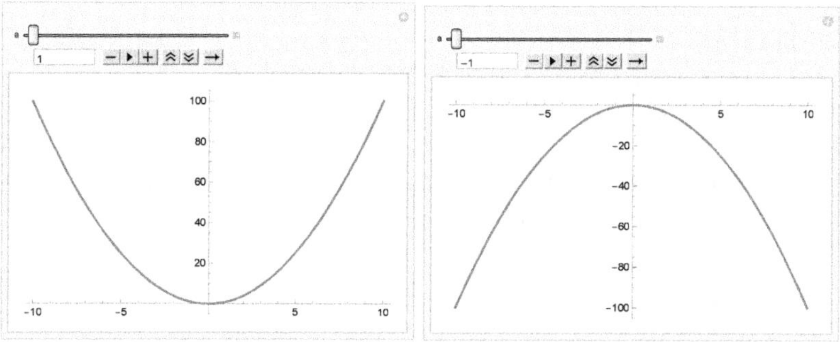

(a) Parabola with a = 1 (b) Parabola for a = −1

Figure A.1: Using `Manipulate` to display parabolas.

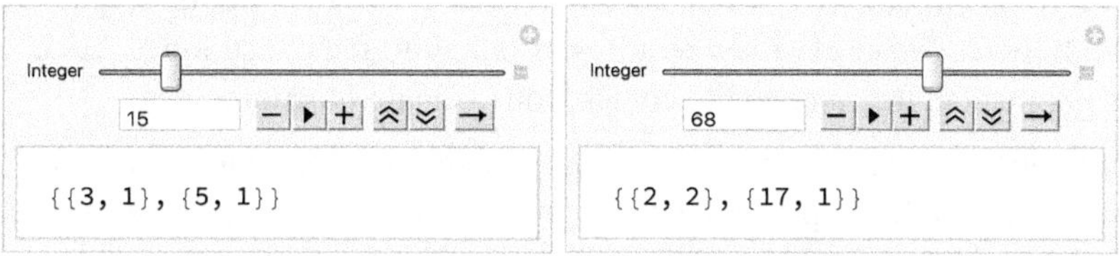

(a) Factoring $15 = 3 \times 5$ (b) Factoring $68 = 2^2 \times 17$

Figure A.2: Using `Manipulate` to display integer factors.

Note that you must tell `Manipulate` to treat `n` as a discrete integer, otherwise `n` would be treated as a continuous real number and the output of `FactorInteger` would be nonsense.

WL also allows for animation of time-varying expressions:

```
Manipulate[
 Plot[Sin[x + t], {x, -2 Pi, 2 Pi}, PlotRange → {-1, 1}],
 {t, 0, 2 Pi}]
```

In Mathematica, this creates an animation of a traveling wave to the right. Figure A.3 shows a glimpse of two snapshots.

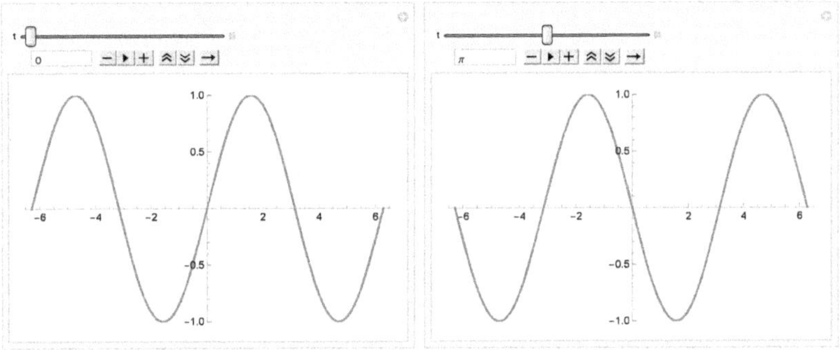

(a) Phase = 0 (b) Phase = π

Figure A.3: Using `Manipulate` to display traveling waves.

In Python, interactivity often means reaching for `ipywidgets`, `plotly`, `Dash`, or `Streamlit`. Each requires installation, setup, and longer code. In Mathematica, the same effect comes from a single function.

`Manipulate` makes dynamic content straightforward. You can visualize a function, simulate a process, or tune model parameters with real-time feedback. Code that would otherwise sit static becomes responsive. This shifts how you explore, prototype, and present ideas, since interactivity is available immediately with almost no effort.

Dynamic Evaluation

Most languages require you to re-run code whenever input values change. In WL, `Dynamic` does that work for you. Wrap a variable or expression, and it stays current as its value changes and no manual refresh is necessary.

```
x = 5; Dynamic[x]
```

which, of course, simply returns `5`. Now change `x = 10`, and the output automatically updates to reflect the new value: `10` in the entire notebook.

You can also pair `Dynamic` with input controls. When you move the slider, the variable `x` changes, and the plot updates in real time. Figure A.4 provides two snapshots of how `Dynamic` and `Slider` work together.

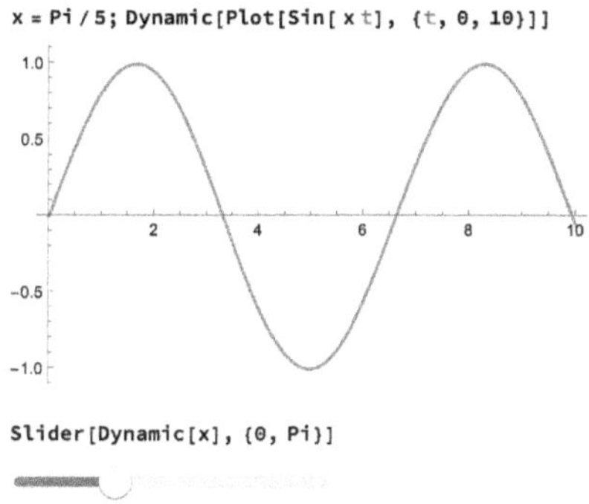

(a) A sinewave

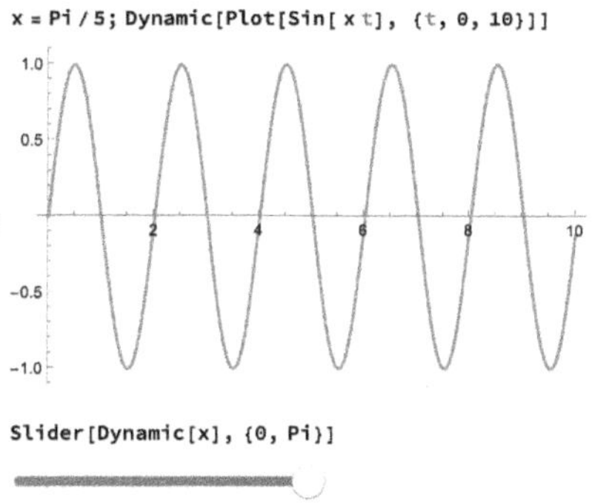

(b) Another sinewave

Figure A.4: Using `Dynamic` for real-time updates to a plot.

In WL, expressions remain current without being re-run by hand, and interfaces update in place as if they were alive. This is the essence of dynamic evaluation. By wrapping code in `Dynamic`, you can create notebooks, simulations, and user interfaces that act more like interactive apps than static scripts. The effect is that instead of writing logic to refresh outputs, you let the system handle it. For anyone used to imperative update loops, this reactive model of computing feels like a new way of exploring, learning, and prototyping.

B Why You Should Write in Mathematica

Even If Everyone Else Is on Python

Let me give it to you straight. If you're a new quant today, chances are someone handed you Python and told you it was the lingua franca of modern finance. And they weren't wrong. Python is everywhere. It's in your bootcamps, in your notebooks, in half the GitHub repos you've cloned but never run. Python is friendly. Python is flexible. Python is free.

But if you asked me what tool actually helps you think like a quant—what lets you explore an idea, see it, tweak it, and push it until it breaks—I wouldn't point you to Python. I'd point you to Mathematica.

Yes, Mathematica. That gorgeous, allegedly expensive, proprietary piece of software most firms won't expense until you ask twice. The one with the weird capitalization and the impossibly elegant typesetting. The one you probably dismissed because your quant friends call it "too academic" or "not production-grade." Ignore them—they're wrong.

I've been in this game for four decades. I've seen tools come and go—FORTRAN, Pascal, APL, Matlab, R, Python, C++, Julia. I've written e^x in assembly and derivative pricing code in C wherever speed and memory were precious. I've debugged complex matrix operations on a Tektronix terminal. I've seen every tool fail under pressure in some way. But Mathematica? Mathematica helped me think.

Let's start with the obvious. Mathematica is beautiful. Not in the aesthetic sense—though yes, the notebook interface still looks like it was designed by someone who's read books with margins—but in the way it mirrors human reasoning. You write code that reads like math. The syntax flows. The function names are legible. No need to load libraries to plot a histogram or set an axis. Your code runs clean, without indentation bugs or version conflicts between `numpy`, `scipy`, and your GPU stack. You're doing math.

That matters, because being a quant means more than writing code. It means engaging with models—testing, refining, and seeing them from every angle. Mathematica lets you do that in one space, in one language, with one mindset. You define your problem, run the simulation, graph the result, and annotate the thought—all in the same page. Need to price an exotic option, simulate a stochastic differential equation, or run a symbolic integration to test a closed-form expression? Mathematica handles it—directly, cleanly, and without hesitation.

Now compare that to Matlab. I know, I know—some of you still use it. Or your boss does. Or that crusty risk model you inherited was built in it. Matlab was fine in the '90s. I used it too.[25] But let's not romanticize it. Matlab is overpriced, clunky, and syntactically awkward. It was built for engineers who needed matrix algebra on the cheap. And it never really evolved. Try doing symbolic math in Matlab. Try building a clean user interface. Try working with non-numeric data structures that aren't cell arrays duct-taped together with `for` loops. It's a relic—stubborn, inflexible, and painfully unaware that it lives in the 21st century.

Mathematica, by contrast, aged well. It kept growing—folding in machine learning, neural nets, GPU support, natural language processing, graph theory, audio and image analysis. And more than just adding features, it made them work together. Seamlessly. In Mathematica, your data can be a symbolic expression, a list of rules, a time series, a graph, or a pixel array—and the same core functions work across them. It's not a zoo of disconnected packages. It's a system.

Python, by contrast, is a Toyota Prius. And I say that with respect. It's reliable. Efficient. Good on gas. The kind of car you loan an intern because it'll probably start in the morning. But no one dreams in or falls in love with a Prius It's a tool for getting from A to B. If your problem is well-defined—if you know exactly which model you want to build, which library handles it, and which cloud function deploys it—Python's great. But the moment you need to explore? To ask, "what if?" and follow that thread into symbolic math, or numerical simulation, or a new functional programming paradigm? Python fragments. You Google. You paste. You refactor. You

[25] In a former life, my company Algorex, Inc. delivered one of the first wireless communications toolboxes to MathWorks.

patch together Stack Overflow advice from three years ago and hope the API hasn't changed. Using Mathematica prevents you from having to cobble together a toolchain. It asks you to think. And then it meets you there.

Let's talk performance. You'll hear the usual digs: *It's not as fast as C.* Or *It's not open-source.* and *It doesn't scale to production.* These criticisms are half-truths at best.

Is it open-source? No. And it never claimed to be. Mathematica is a Bentley — engineered, complete, and ready to drive. You don't tinker with a DIY kit. You just use it, and it works. Every time. And if your quant research group or employer can't afford a Mathematica license, then you've got bigger problems than tool selection. You don't run Monte Carlo on a shoestring. You don't optimize risk models on goodwill. The real cost is your time—and the risk of misunderstanding your model.

Is it fast? Fast enough. For prototyping, exploratory modeling, symbolic derivation, and visualization? It's more than fast—it's fluent. And when you hit performance limits, you can compile. You can link C libraries. You can push things to GPU. You can even call Python if you must.

The truth is, Mathematica never binds itself to a single field. It's built for fluency across many. It's more than a math tool—it's a platform for thinking. You can model interest rate curves, simulate partial differential equations, build interactive dashboards, test statistical assumptions, and even generate LaTeX-ready reports—all in the same file. Try doing that in Jupyter without losing a day to config files and broken extensions.

Keep Python close—you'll use it often. R will have its place too, especially when factor regressions come up in portfolio meetings. But make Mathematica your base—that's the space where your real computational thinking starts. No need to wait for team approval. Use Mathematica for your own work—for your own clarity. Turn to it when you're stuck, when you need to see the structure of a problem. Use it when you want your tools to open paths. Because when you're chasing alpha in a nonlinear world, what clarity matters beyond just speed. And Mathematica gives you clarity.

Buy the license. Ask forgiveness later. You'll thank me.

My First Encounter with Mathematica

In 1986, I was working at Teknekron Corporation, a UC Berkeley spinoff located at 2121 Allston Way in downtown Berkeley. Teknekron was more than a tech outfit. It was a deeptech venture foundry before the term even existed. We spun out software and systems companies rooted in university research, and we did it with the kind of academic restlessness that never quite trusted the status quo. I was deep into digital signal processing and microprocessor-based systems, and always on the lookout for tools that cut closer to the metal, or made math behave.

So when the NeXT Computer was announced—Jobs' sleek magnesium cube promising Unix brains and object-oriented muscle—I ordered one. This was around 1988, when the machine finally shipped. (Johnson, 1989; Paul, 1995) It arrived with a keyboard that felt engineered, a mouse that behaved, and an operating system that looked like science fiction compared to DOS. But what really mattered was the software it shipped with: Mathematica 1.1, from a young Stephen Wolfram. (Wolfram, 2013, 2016)

Let's see if Mathematica can bend time!

That changed everything.

I had been writing math code in FORTRAN and C, trying to tame equations and run simulations with the blunt tools of the day. Mathematica felt different. It was a symbolic engine, a numerical solver, and a new language for computational thinking. I could model systems, visualize results, and experiment with symbolic algebra all in one place. The moment I saw a differential equation rendered and solved interactively on screen, From the start, it was clear: this was a full platform for thinking in math—precisely, interactively, and without friction.

But not everything shimmered. The machine looked like it had landed from the future, but the hardware reminded you it still came through a shipping dock. I remember the moment I unboxed the monitor—expecting something sleek, maybe even flat, based on the glossy photos and Steve Jobs' usual flourish. Instead, what I got was a Philips CRT in a stylish black case. Heavy (about 27 Kg). Clunky. Grayscale. The thing felt like it had been repurposed from a submarine console. Elegant design on the outside, but inside—still a tube.

I called NeXT to ask about it. The sales rep more or less told me: "That's what we ship." Not exactly the Apple Store experience.

Still, I kept the machine and put it to all kinds of good use. The power of Mathematica far outweighed the bulk of the monitor. It became my daily environment for modeling, exploring signal processing algorithms, and later, financial systems. While others were still typing code into terminals and plotting on dot-matrix printers, I had something that looked and felt like the future.

In hindsight, that early encounter shaped the way I think about tools. It taught me that a platform—when done right—can change how you work, how you reason, even how you model reality. It also reminded me that form factors age faster than ideas. The NeXT monitor was obsolete in a few years. The language of Mathematica still runs through my work, decades later.

Who Uses Mathematica?

Some of the sharpest minds in quantitative finance—and a few beyond it—have made Mathematica a key part of how they think. They use it because it helps them see ideas in action. The goal is discovery, shaping ideas. For testing models in motion.

Scholarly Super Quant: Nassim Nicholas Taleb Taleb, the former options trader turned philosopher of risk, is best known for *The Black Swan* and his ongoing critique of Gaussian-based models. But behind the writing is a deeply technical thinker. He uses Mathematica for symbolic math, probability theory, Monte Carlo simulation, and visualizing the non-Gaussian structures that underpin his work (Taleb, 2020). He's said the software helps him express ideas that are difficult to capture in Python or R—especially when dealing with fat tails, power laws, and dynamic systems. His notebooks, written entirely in Mathematica, reflect his voice: dense, sharp-edged, and exacting.

Vineer Bhansali: Physicist Turned Bond Trader Vineer Bhansali, founder of LongTail Alpha and former head of portfolio management at PIMCO, has a similarly long relationship with the tool (Bhansali, 2013). Trained as a physicist and seasoned as a trader, Bhansali is known for combining rigorous quant modeling with an awareness of human behavior. In books like *Tail Risk Hedging* and *Fixed Income Finance: A Quantitative Approach*, he credits Mathematica as his prototyping platform. (Bhansali, 2010) It's what he uses to build models, run tests, and stress ideas—especially when the market backdrop is volatile or unstable. For him, it's a tool for reasoning through complexity.

Both have plenty of options. They can use any stack they choose. They work in Mathematica because it lets them move fast, think clearly, and stay close to the math. They use it the way it's meant to be used: to push on ideas until they reveal their shape.

The Tale of an Odd Duck: Seth Chandler, the Mathematica Lawyer Seth J. Chandler is something of an outlier. A law professor at the University of Houston, he writes legal scholarship using Mathematica. Not Excel. Not Word. Not R. *Mathematica.* He works outside finance, but brings a quant's sensibility to law. When asked why he uses the software, Chandler gave a simple answer: "Because I'd like to show there's science behind what I say."

That's a rare case in legal writing—and not exactly common in finance either. Chandler builds legal models the way a seasoned quant might build pricing trees: with logic, clarity, and structure you can interrogate. His work touches on insurance regulation, health policy, and rule-based systems, often using simulation and symbolic methods to make abstract legal ideas behave like systems.

Chandler does something truly unique: he makes law "computational." And he uses Mathematica to clarify—to expose conflicting rules, distorted incentives, and arguments that collapse under scrutiny. He's a lawyer, yes. But he thinks like a quant. Which is why his code, and his reasoning, run clean. (Chandler, 2023)

C Mathematica Code Snippets

Chapter 3

Listing C.1: Code for Figure 3.1a

```
SeedRandom[12345];
dataGBM =
  RandomFunction[
   GeometricBrownianMotionProcess[0, .1, 1], {0, 1, 0.01}];

ListLinePlot[dataGBM, PlotTheme → "Monochrome",
 PlotMarkers → "",
 BaseStyle → {FontFamily → "Latin␣Modern␣Roman",
 FontSize → 11},
 Frame → True]
```

Listing C.2: Code for Figure 3.1b

```
SeedRandom[54321]; mertonP =
 TransformedProcess[(μ - σ²/2) t + σ w[t] + j[t],
  {w ≈ WienerProcess[0, σ],
   j ≈ CompoundPoissonProcess
     [λ, NormalDistribution[0, σ]]}, t];

logData = RandomFunction[mertonP /.
    {μ → 0.2, σ → 0.7, λ → 3}, {0, 1, 0.01}, 2];

priceData = TimeSeriesMap[ # &, Exp[logData]];
ListLinePlot[priceData, PlotStyle → Thick,
 PlotTheme → "Monochrome", Frame → True,
 PlotMarkers → "",
 BaseStyle → {FontFamily → "Latin␣Modern␣Roman",
   FontSize → 10}]
```

Listing C.3: Code for Figure 3.3

```
SeedRandom[1235]; (* For reproducibility *)

(* Generate jumps *)
mertonJumps = RandomVariate[NormalDistribution[0, 0.05],
    1000];
kouJumps =
  Table[If[
    RandomReal[] < 0.7, -RandomVariate[ExponentialDistribution
        [0.1]],
    RandomVariate[ExponentialDistribution[0.05]]], {1000}];

(* Histogram for Merton *)
mertonHist =
  Histogram[mertonJumps, {-0.2, 0.2, 0.01}, "PDF", ChartStyle
      → Gray,
    AxesLabel → {"Size", "Counts"}, PlotLabel → "Merton",
   Epilog → {Dashed, Line[{{-0.1, 0}, {-0.1, 10}}],
     Line[{{0.1, 0}, {0.1, 10}}], Line[{{0, 0}, {0, 10}}]},
   BaseStyle → {FontFamily → "Latin␣Modern␣Roman",
   FontSize → 11},
   PlotTheme → "Monochrome"];

(* Histogram for Kou *)
kouHist =
  Histogram[kouJumps, {-0.2, 0.2, 0.01}, "PDF", ChartStyle →
      Gray,
   AxesLabel → {"Size", "Counts"}, PlotLabel → "Kou",
   PlotTheme → "Monochrome",
   Epilog → {Dashed, Line[{{-0.1, 0}, {-0.1, 10}}],
     Line[{{0.1, 0}, {0.1, 10}}], Line[{{0, 0}, {0, 10}}]},
   BaseStyle → {FontFamily → "Latin␣Modern␣Roman",
   FontSize → 11}];

(* Display side by side *)
GraphicsRow[{mertonHist, kouHist}]
```

Listing C.4: Code for Figure 3.4

```
DateListPlot[glddata = FinancialData["GLD", "Close",
"Jan.␣1,␣2024"], PlotTheme → "Monochrome",
PlotMarkers → "",
BaseStyle → {FontFamily → "Latin␣Modern␣Roman",
FontSize → 11}]

DateListPlot[spydata = FinancialData["SPY", "Close",
"Jan.␣1,␣2024"], PlotTheme → "Monochrome",
PlotMarkers → "",
BaseStyle → {FontFamily → "Latin␣Modern␣Roman",
FontSize → 11}]
```

Listing C.5: Code for Figure 3.5

```
DateListPlot[gldret = FinancialData["GLD", "Return",
"Jan.␣1,␣2024"], PlotTheme → "Monochrome",
PlotMarkers → "",
BaseStyle → {FontFamily → "Latin␣Modern␣Roman",
FontSize → 11}]

DateListPlot[spyret = FinancialData["SPY", "Return",
"Jan.␣1,␣2024"], PlotTheme → "Monochrome",
PlotMarkers → "",
BaseStyle → {FontFamily → "Latin␣Modern␣Roman",
FontSize → 11}]
```

Listing C.6: Code for Figure 3.6

```
SmoothHistogram[gldret, PlotTheme → "Monochrome",
BaseStyle → {FontFamily → "Latin␣Modern␣Roman",
FontSize → 11}]

SmoothHistogram[spyret, PlotTheme → "Monochrome",
BaseStyle → {FontFamily → "Latin␣Modern␣Roman",
FontSize → 11}]
```

Listing C.7: Code for Figure 3.7

```
QuantilePlot[spyret["Values"]["Magnitudes"],
 PlotRange → Full,
 PlotStyle → Black,
 BaseStyle → {FontFamily → "Latin␣Modern␣Roman",
 FontSize → 11}]

QuantilePlot[gldret["Values"]["Magnitudes"],
 PlotRange → Full,
 PlotStyle → Black,
 BaseStyle → {FontFamily → "Latin␣Modern␣Roman",
 FontSize → 11}]
```

Chapter 5

Listing C.8: Code for Figure 5.1

```
DateListPlot[djicrash1 =
  FinancialData["DJI", "Close", {{1987, 1, 1}, {1988, 1, 1}}],
 PlotTheme → "Monochrome", PlotMarkers → "",
 BaseStyle → {FontFamily → "Latin␣Modern␣Roman",
 FontSize → 11},
 FrameTicks → {{None, None}, {Automatic, None}}]

 DateListPlot[djicrash2 =
  FinancialData["DJI", "Close", {{1998, 1, 1}, {1999, 1, 1}}],
 PlotTheme → "Monochrome", PlotMarkers → "",
 BaseStyle → {FontFamily → "Latin␣Modern␣Roman",
 FontSize → 11},
 FrameTicks → {{None, None}, {Automatic, None}}]

 DateListPlot[djicrash3 =
  FinancialData["DJI", "Close", {{2008, 1, 1}, {2009, 1, 1}}],
 PlotTheme → "Monochrome", PlotMarkers → "",
 BaseStyle → {FontFamily → "Latin␣Modern␣Roman",
 FontSize → 11} ,
 FrameTicks → {{None, None}, {Automatic, None}}]

 DateListPlot[djicrash4 =
  FinancialData["DJI", "Close", {{2020, 1, 1}, {2021, 1, 1}}],
 PlotTheme → "Monochrome", PlotMarkers → "",
 BaseStyle → {FontFamily → "Latin␣Modern␣Roman",
 FontSize → 11},
 FrameTicks → {{None, None}, {Automatic, None}}]
```

Listing C.9: Code for Figure 5.2

```
(* pull the data *)
djiCrash = FinancialData["DJI", "Close", {{1987, 1, 1}, {1988,
     1, 1}}];

(* Extract raw data from TimeSeries object *)
data = Normal[djiCrash];

(* Define target dates *)
peakDate = {1987, 8, 25};
troughDate = {1987, 10, 19};

(* Find points matching those dates *)
peakPt = SelectFirst[data, DateList[#[[1]]][[;; 3]] ==
     peakDate &];
troughPt = SelectFirst[data, DateList[#[[1]]][[;; 3]] ==
     troughDate &];

DateListPlot[djicrash1, PlotTheme → "Monochrome",
 PlotMarkers → None,
 BaseStyle → {FontFamily → "Latin␣Modern␣Roman", FontSize →
     11},
 FrameTicks → {{None, None}, {Automatic, None}},
 Epilog → {Text[Style["\[FilledCircle]", 14], peakPt, {0,
     -0.75}],
   Text[Style["\[CircleTimes]", 14], troughPt, {0, 0.5}]}]
```

Listing C.10: Code for Table 5.1

```
(*  Collect two years of Dow Jones Index closing prices *)
(*  Data has elements like {{Y,M,D},value} *)
rawData = FinancialData["DJI", "Close",
   {{1986, 1, 1}, {1988, 1, 1}}, Method → "Legacy"];

(* Convert to {DateObject,value} *)
data = {DateObject[#1], #2} & @@@ rawData;

(* Filter last 1 year of data *)
endDate = Max[data[[All, 1]]];
oneYearAgo = endDate - Quantity[1, "Years"];
lastYearData = Select[data, #[[1]] >= oneYearAgo &];
(* Extract date and value vectors *)
dates = lastYearData[[All, 1]];
values = lastYearData[[All, 2]];
(* Compute running peak *)
runningPeak = FoldList[Max, First[values], Rest[values]];
```

```
(* Compute drawdown *)
drawdowns = 1 - values/runningPeak;
(* Max drawdown and positions *)
maxDD = Max[drawdowns];
maxPos = First@Ordering[drawdowns, -1];

(* Trough and peak info *)
troughDate = dates[[maxPos]];
troughValue = values[[maxPos]];
peakIndex = First@FirstPosition[values[[;; maxPos]],
    runningPeak[[maxPos]]];
peakDate = dates[[peakIndex]];
peakValue = values[[peakIndex]];
(* Recovery info (if any) *)
recoveryIndex =
  SelectFirst[Range[maxPos + 1, Length[values]],
   values[[#]] >= runningPeak[[maxPos]] &];
recoveryDate = If[MissingQ[recoveryIndex],
   "Not␣Recovered", dates[[recoveryIndex]]];
recoveryDuration = If[MissingQ[recoveryIndex],
   "N/A", recoveryIndex - peakIndex];

(* Output summary *)
(* Convert Association to table format and display *)
summary = <|"Max␣Drawdown␣(\%)" → N[100*maxDD],
   "Peak␣Date" → peakDate,
   "Peak␣Value" → peakValue,
   "Trough␣Date" → troughDate,
   "Trough␣Value" → troughValue,
   "Recovery␣Date" → recoveryDate,
   "Drawdown␣Duration␣(days)" → recoveryDuration|>;

summary // Normal // TableForm
```

Chapter 6

Listing C.11: Code for Figure 6.3a

```
pdata = FinancialData["SP500", "Close",
   {{2020, 1, 1}, {2021, 1, 1}}];
DateListPlot[pdata, PlotRange → Full,
 PlotTheme → "Monochrome", PlotMarkers → "",
 BaseStyle → {FontFamily → "Latin␣Modern␣Roman",
   FontSize → 11}]
```

Listing C.12: Code for Figure 6.3b

```
(* Input:daily closing prices for one year *)
pdata = FinancialData["SP500", "Close",
   {{2020, 1, 1}, {2021, 1, 1}}];
prices = pdata["Values"];

(* Compute daily log returns via Differences *)
logReturns = Differences[Log[prices]];

(* Set the number of jackknife replicates *)
M = 5000;

(* Jackknife function *)
jackknifeAnnualReturn[lr_List, dropIdx_List] :=
  Module[{posToDrop, reducedLogSum},
   posToDrop = List /@ dropIdx;(* {{i1},{i2}} *)
   reducedLogSum = Total[Delete[lr, posToDrop]];
   Exp[reducedLogSum] - 1];

(* Generate M jackknife samples *)
n = Length[logReturns];
jackknifeSamples =
  Table[Module[{excluded = RandomSample[Range[n], 2]},
    jackknifeAnnualReturn[logReturns, excluded]], {M}];

(*  compute the 1%,median,99% quantiles *)
qs = Quantile[jackknifeSamples, {0.01, 0.5, 0.99}];

(*  build a smooth kernel distribution *)
dist = SmoothKernelDistribution[jackknifeSamples];

SmoothHistogram[jackknifeSamples, PlotRange → Full,
 PlotTheme → "Monochrome",
 BaseStyle → {FontFamily → "Latin␣Modern␣Roman",
   FontSize → 11},
```

```
(* hide the y axis line *)
AxesStyle → {Automatic,
  Transparent},
Ticks → {Automatic, None},
Epilog → {(* dashed gray lines at 10% and 90% *) {Dashed,
    Gray,
   InfiniteLine[{{qs[[1]], 0}, {qs[[1]], 1}}],
   InfiniteLine[{{qs[[3]], 0}, {qs[[3]], 1}}]},
  (* Mark points at min, median, max with labels *)
  {Black, PointSize[Large], Point[{min, PDF[dist, min]}],
   Text["min", {min, PDF[dist, min]}, {0, -1.5}],
   Point[{qs[[2]], PDF[dist, qs[[2]]]}],
   Text["med", {qs[[2]], PDF[dist, qs[[2]]]}, {-1.5, -1.0}],
   Point[{max, PDF[dist, max]}],
   Text["max", {max, PDF[dist, max]}, {0, -1.5}]}
  }]
```

Chapter 7

Listing C.13: Code for Algorithm 1

```
(*  Collect two years of Dow Jones Index *)
rawData = FinancialData["DJI", "Close",
   {{1986, 1, 1}, {1988, 1, 1}}, Method → "Legacy"];
(* Convert to {DateObject,value} *)
data = {DateObject[#1], #2} & @@@ rawData;
endDate = Max[data[[All, 1]]];
oneYearAgo = endDate - Quantity[1, "Years"];
lastYearData = Select[data, #[[1]] >= oneYearAgo &];
dates = lastYearData[[All, 1]];
values = lastYearData[[All, 2]];
runningPeak = FoldList[Max, First[values],
Rest[values]];
drawdowns = 1 - values/runningPeak;
(* Max drawdown and positions *)
maxDD = Max[drawdowns];
maxPos = First@Ordering[drawdowns, -1];
troughDate = dates[[maxPos]];
troughValue = values[[maxPos]];
peakIndex = First@FirstPosition[values[[;; maxPos]],
    runningPeak[[maxPos]]];
peakDate = dates[[peakIndex]];
peakValue = values[[peakIndex]];
(* Recovery info (if any) *)
recoveryIndex =
  SelectFirst[Range[maxPos + 1, Length[values]],
   values[[#]] >= runningPeak[[maxPos]] &];
recoveryDate = If[MissingQ[recoveryIndex],
   "Not␣Recovered", dates[[recoveryIndex]]];
recoveryDuration = If[MissingQ[recoveryIndex],
   "N/A", recoveryIndex - peakIndex];

(* Output summary *)
(* Convert Association to table format and display *)
summary = <|"Max␣Drawdown␣(\%)" → N[100*maxDD],
   "Peak␣Date" → peakDate,
   "Peak␣Value" → peakValue,
   "Trough␣Date" → troughDate,
   "Trough␣Value" → troughValue,
   "Recovery␣Date" → recoveryDate,
   "Drawdown␣Duration␣(days)" → recoveryDuration|>;
summary // Normal // TableForm
```

Listing C.14: Code for Figure 7.1a

```
Plot[Sqrt[x^2 + 1] - 1, {x, 0, 10^-8},
 PlotPoints → 50,
 PlotRange → {{0, 10^-8}, {0, 5*10^-17}}, PlotTheme → "
     Monochrome",
 BaseStyle → {FontFamily → "Latin␣Modern␣Roman",
  → 11}]
```

Listing C.15: Code for Figure 7.1b

```
Plot[x^2/(Sqrt[x^2 + 1] + 1), {x, 0, 10^-8},
PlotPoints → 50,
 PlotRange → {{0, 10^-8}, {0, 5*10^-17}}, PlotTheme → "
     Monochrome",
 BaseStyle → {FontFamily → "Latin␣Modern␣Roman",
 FontSize → 11}]
```

Glossary

Almgren-Chriss Model A framework for optimal trade execution under market impact and risk constraints.

Alpha A measure of performance on a risk-adjusted basis, ing the excess return of an investment relative to a benchmark.

Arbitrage The simultaneous purchase and sale of similar assets to secure a risk-free profit from price differences.

Avellaneda-Stoikov Model A high-frequency trading model balancing quote aggressiveness with inventory risk.

Black-Scholes Model A mathematical model for pricing options, assuming log-normal distribution of asset prices and no arbitrage.

Brownian Motion A continuous-time stochastic process modeling asset prices in financial theory.

Conditional Value-at-Risk (CVaR) Expected loss given that the loss is beyond the Value-at-Risk threshold.

Execution Risk The risk of loss from slippage or adverse price movements during trade execution.

Gaussian Copula A method for modeling dependence structures in multivariate distributions, especially in credit risk.

Geometric Brownian Motion A log-normal model for asset price evolution used in Black-Scholes.

Heston Model A stochastic volatility model used to better capture real market dynamics.

High Frequency Trading Trading strategies that rely on ultra-fast execution and high turnover.

Inventory Risk The risk associated with holding large positions, particularly in market-making.

Ito's Lemma A fundamental result in stochastic calculus used to determine the differential of a function of a stochastic process.

Jackknife Sampling A resampling method used to assess the stability of performance metrics (e.g., annual return, Sharpe ratio) in financial models by repeatedly recalculating them after removing one or more observations. Helps detect sensitivity to outliers and estimate bias in backtest results.

Jump Diffusion Model An extension of GBM that includes sudden price jumps.

Liquidity The ease with which an asset can be bought or sold in the market without affecting its price.

Long Short-Term Memory A type of neural network designed to learn patterns—whether in speech or text—by remembering what matters and forgetting what doesn't.

Long Tails Distributions where extreme values occur more frequently than in the normal distribution. Also called Fat Tails.

Look Ahead Bias A pitfall in backtesting where future information is inadvertently used in the analysis.

Market Microstructure The study of trading mechanics, order types, and the behavior of market participants.

Markov Chain	A stochastic process that transitions between states with probabilities that depend only on the current state, not on the path taken to reach it.
Markov Chain Monte Carlo (MCMC)	A class of algorithms for sampling from probability distributions based on constructing a Markov chain.
Maximum Drawdown	The largest observed loss from a portfolio's peak value to its subsequent trough before a new peak is reached.
Mean Reversion	The tendency of prices to move back towards their long-term average.
Model Risk	The risk of loss arising from errors in model design, implementation, or use.
Monte Carlo Simulation	A computational technique that uses random sampling to approximate complex mathematical models.
Moral Hazard	A situation where one party takes on more risk because another party bears the consequences of that risk.
Options Greeks	Sensitivity measures of option prices to various risk factors.
Overfitting	When a model fits the training data too closely, capturing noise rather than underlying patterns.
Path Dependency	A property of some derivatives where the payoff depends on the sequence of underlying asset prices, not just the final price.
Portfolio Optimization	The process of choosing the proportions of various assets to include in a portfolio, balancing risk and return.
QQ Plot	Compares your data's quantiles to those of a normal distribution, mapping them point by point. If the data is truly normal, the dots will trace a tidy 45-degree line.
Quantitative Easing	A monetary policy where a central bank buys securities to increase the money supply and encourage lending and investment.

Random Walk A path that consists of a succession of random steps, often used to model asset price movements.

Risk-Neutral Measure A probability measure where all investors are indifferent to risk, simplifying pricing in derivatives.

Robustness The ability of a model or system to perform well under a variety of conditions.

Sharpe Ratio A measure of risk-adjusted return, calculated as the excess return over the risk-free rate divided by the standard deviation of returns.

Stochastic Alpha-Beta-Rho A stochastic volatility model used to describe the evolution of forward prices and their implied volatilities, particularly for pricing and hedging interest rate and foreign exchange derivatives.

Stochastic Volatility A situation where the volatility of a variable, such as an asset price, changes over time in an unpredictable manner.

Stress Testing The process of evaluating a system's ability to withstand adverse market conditions.

Tail Risk The risk of extreme price movements at the ends of a distribution of returns.

Value-at-Risk (VaR) A statistical measure of the potential loss in value of a portfolio over a given time period for a set confidence interval.

Volatility Clustering The phenomenon where large changes in asset prices tend to be followed by more large changes.

Volatility Smile A pattern in which implied volatility differs across options with different strike prices.

Zero-Coupon Bond A bond that does not pay periodic interest but is sold at a discount to its face value.

Bibliography

Acton, Forman S. 2005. *Real computing made real: Preventing errors in scientific and engineering calculations*. Courier Corporation.

Acton, Forman S. 2020. *Numerical methods that work*, Vol. 2. American Mathematical Soc..

Almgren, Robert, and Neil Chriss. 2001. Optimal execution of portfolio transactions. *Journal of Risk* 3: 5–40.

Augustin, Patrick, Ing-Haw Cheng, and Ludovic Van den Bergen. 2021. Volmageddon and the failure of short volatility products. *Financial Analysts Journal* 77 (3): 35–51.

Austin, Robert D., and Darren Meister. 2015. Knight Capital Americas LLC. Harvard Business School Case Study. Product #: W15077-PDF-ENG.

Berger, Yves G, and Chris J Skinner. 2005. A jackknife variance estimator for unequal probability sampling. *Journal of the Royal Statistical Society Series B: Statistical Methodology* 67 (1): 79–89.

Bhansali, Vineer. 2010. *Fixed income finance: A quantitative approach*. New York: McGraw-Hill.

Bhansali, Vineer. 2013. *Tail risk hedging: Creating robust portfolios for volatile markets*. McGraw Hill Professional.

Chandler, Seth J. 2023. *Query: Getting information from data with the wolfram language*. Champaign, IL: Wolfram Media, Inc..

Derman, Emanuel. 2012. *My life as a quant: reflections on physics and finance*. John Wiley & Sons.

Fletcher, Laurence, and Richard Henderson. 2020. Turbulent markets upend volatility hedge funds. *Financial Times*. `https://www.ft.com/content/b8ddbf92-c9b4-4a81-a167-ef9ee80962a5`.

Gilli, Manfred, Dietmar Maringer, and Enrico Schumann. 2019. *Numerical methods and optimization in finance*. Academic Press.

Hull, John C. 2012. *Options, futures, and other derivatives*, 8th edn. Upper Saddle River, NJ: Prentice Hall.

Hull, John C. 2023. *Risk management and financial institutions*. John Wiley & Sons.

Johnson, James W. 1989. The NeXT Generation of Computer Technology JSTOR.

Kou, Steve G. 2007. Jump-diffusion models for asset pricing in financial engineering. *Handbooks in operations research and management science* 15: 73–116.

Lindsey, Richard R, and Barry Schachter. 2009. *How i became a quant: Insights from 25 of wall street's elite*. John Wiley & Sons.

Merton, Robert C. 1976. Option pricing when underlying stock returns are discontinuous. *Journal of financial economics* 3 (1-2): 125–144.

Paul, C Abbott. 1995. Mathematica. In *Revival: The handbook of software for engineers and scientists*, 926–962. CRC Press.

Savage, Sam L, and Harry M Markowitz. 2009. *The flaw of averages: Why we underestimate risk in the face of uncertainty*. John Wiley & Sons.

Taleb, Nassim Nicholas. 2020. *Statistical consequences of fat tails: Real world preasymptotics, epistemology, and applications*. STEM Academic Press.

Wolfram, Stephen. 2013. Remembering Richard Crandall (1947–2012) ACM New York, NY, USA.

Wolfram, Stephen. 2016. *Idea makers: personal perspectives on the lives & ideas of some notable people*. Wolfram Media.

Index

Acton, Forman S, 65
AI, 77, 80–84
Almgren–Chriss Model, 30, 31
Alpha, 5, 29, 31, 55, 77, 84
Arithmetic Mean, 88–91
Assumption, 5, 9, 29, 53
Avellaneda–Stoikov Model, 31, 32
Average, 87, 88, 90–94

Backtest, 5, 29, 31, 51, 52, 54, 55, 74, 101
Bhansali, Vineer, 122
Bias, 52, 53, 55, 81, 83
Bitcoin, 58–60
Black-Scholes, 4, 10, 15
Brownian Motion, 1, 16, 17

Chandler, Seth J., 122
Covid Pandemic, 40, 62, 84
Crash, 16, 20, 24, 25
CVaR, 45

DJIA, 40, 42
Drawdown, 42

ETF, 22
Ex-ante, 44
Ex-post, 44

Fund of Funds, 91

Gammon Capital, 84
Gaussian Copula, 38, 39
GBM, 15–17, 19
Geometric Mean, 89, 90, 92
Gold, 21–23

Harmonic Mean, 90, 93
High Frequency Trading, 31

Jackknife Sampling, 62

Knight Capital, 9, 38
Kou Jump Model, 20, 26

Latency, 31, 32, 35, 52, 56, 81
Liquidity, 4, 10, 16, 17, 24–26, 28–30, 33, 35, 38–40, 51, 53, 98
Long Tails, 21, 23–25
LSTM, 34, 80
LTCM, 4, 39

Mathematica, 119–122
Max Drawdown, 40, 42, 43
Merton Jump Diffusion Model, 17, 18, 20
Monte Carlo Simulation, 3, 44, 102, 119, 121

NeXT Computer, 120

Optimization, 54, 55

PnL, 5, 105

Psychology, 12, 37, 46, 47
Python, 117–119

QQ Plot, 24

Regimes, 57–59, 64
Risk, 4, 37–39, 46, 47

S&P500, 24, 62
SABR, 3, 16
SDE, 3, 7, 25
Sharpe Ratio, 5, 27, 30, 54
Slippage, 3, 29, 30, 51–53, 56
Stochastic, 1, 4, 6, 7, 25, 73, 93, 99, 104
Survivorship, 52, 53

Tail Event, 24
Taleb, Nassim Nicholas, 121
Teknekron, 119
Theft, 96, 97
Trader, 5, 7, 9, 12, 20, 27, 28, 30, 33, 35, 46, 47, 81, 83, 84, 98, 99
Transaction Cost, 4, 53, 56

VaR, 2, 23, 39, 43, 45, 46, 80
Volatility, 4, 5, 7, 10, 11, 15, 16, 20, 24, 32–35, 37, 38, 40, 47, 52, 54, 71, 74, 77, 81, 104, 105
Volmageddon, 28

Wolfram Language, 107, 108, 110, 115
Wolfram, Stephen, 120

XAI, 82